Time Stages 1 & 2 and Background information

A Unit for teachers

Published for the Schools Council by
Macdonald Educational, London and New York

© Schools Council Publications 1972

First impression 1972
Second impression (with amendments) 1973
Third impression (with amendments) 1974

ISBN 0 356 04008 9

Published by
Macdonald Educational
49-50 Poland Street
London W1

850 Seventh Avenue
New York 10019

The chief author of this book:

Roy Richards

The other members of the Science 5/13 team:

Len Ennever   Project Director

Albert James   Deputy Project Director

Wynne Harlen   Evaluator

Sheila Parker
Don Radford
Mary Horn

Made and printed by Waterlow (Dunstable) Limited

General preface

'Science 5/13' is a Project sponsored jointly by the Schools Council, the Nuffield Foundation and the Scottish Education Department, and based at the University of Bristol School of Education. It aims at helping teachers to help children between the ages of five and thirteen years to learn science through first-hand experience using a variety of methods.

The Project produces books that comprise Units dealing with subject-areas in which children are likely to conduct investigations. Some of these Units are supported by books of background information. The Units are linked by objectives that the Project team hopes children will attain through their work. The aims of the Project are explained in a general guide for teachers called *With objectives in mind,* which contains the Project's guide to Objectives for children learning science, reprinted at the back of each Unit.

Acknowledgements

The Project is deeply grateful to its many friends:
to the local education authorities who have
helped us work in their areas, to those of their staff
who, acting as area representatives, have borne
the heavy brunt of administering our trials, and to
the teachers, heads and wardens who have been
generous without stint in working with their
children on our materials. The books we have
written drew substance from the work they did
for us, and it was through their critical appraisal
that our materials reached their present form. For
guidance, we had our sponsors, our Consultative
Committee and, for support, in all our working,
the University of Bristol. To all of them we
acknowledge our many debts : their help has been
invaluable.

Metrication

This has given us a great deal to think about. We
have been given much good advice by
well-informed friends, and we have consulted
many reports by learned bodies. Following the
advice and the reports wherever possible we have
expressed quantities in metric units with Imperial
units afterwards in square brackets if it seemed
useful to state them so. There are, however, some
cases to which the recommendations are difficult
to apply. For instance we have difficulty with units
such as miles per hour (which has statutory force
in this country and with some Imperial units that
are still in current use for common commodities
and, as far as we know, liable to remain so for some
time. In these cases we have tried to use our
common sense, and, in order to make statements
that are both accurate and helpful to teachers we
have quoted Imperial measures followed by the
approximate metric equivalent in square brackets
if it seemed sensible to give them. Where we have
quoted statements made by children, or given
illustrations that are children's work, we have left
unaltered the units in which the children worked—
in any case some of these units were arbitrary.

Contents

Introduction

What is time ?
—'the interval between two events' ?
—'a limited stretch of continued existence' ?

Time is a difficult concept to grasp. Perhaps something of its elusiveness is revealed in the following story attributed to Professor George Harrison.

'A certain retired sea captain made his home in a secluded spot on the island of Zanzibar. As a sentimental reminder of his seafaring career he still had his ship's chronometer and religiously kept it wound and in good operating condition. Every day, exactly at noon, as indicated on his chronometer, he observed the ritual of firing off a volley from a small cannon. On one rare occasion he received a visit from an old friend who inquired how the captain verified the correctness of his chronometer. "Oh," he replied, "there is a horologist over there in the town of Zanzibar where I go whenever I lay in supplies. He has very reliable time and as I have fairly frequent occasion to go that way I almost always walk past his window and check my time against his." After his visit was over the visitor dropped into the horologist's shop and inquired how the horologist checked his time. "Oh," replied he, "there's an old sea captain over on the other end of the island who, I am told, is quite a fanatic about accurate time and who shoots off a gun every day exactly at noon, so I always check my time and correct it by his".'*

---

*   *Story told by Cohen, Crowe and Dumond who attribute it to Professor George Harrison (reproduced by permission of the publishers, John Wiley, Interscience Ltd.)*

The material in this Unit stresses those activities concerned with the scientific aspects of time. It shows how children gather an increasing awareness of the duration of events ; the delight they take in making clocks, using water, shadows, candles, sand, pendulums or the stars themselves. It also shows how, for example, the phases of the moon and day and night may be looked at.

It is hoped that the Unit will convey much more. Time is a very broadly based topic and, tackled by any group of children in a spirit of inquiry, it will lead them into many fields of knowledge. It also stirs the imagination and leads very many children to good creative writing and poetry.

The Moon
The melon-sliced moon
Like a queen in armour with a lance of light
Spreading her silken wings to cover all living things.
Gliding gracefully through the inky sky,
A maiden playing hide-and-seek
She has her phases.
First a silvery bow appears
Followed soon by half her face
She gaily swims in the darkness above
Like a silver dace
In the Avon.

Junior Boy

Finally, the text contains background information which both supports the activities suggested in the text and puts forward further fields for study.

A classroom situation

This section contains a description of work from a class of eight-year-olds in just one school. This particular example is not set out because it is unusual, or even perhaps especially worthy of mention, but because it is a good example of the sorts of situations that might arise from a topic such as Time.

The work on time began with a display. The teacher had collected a lot of old clocks, few of which worked, and arranged them against a backcloth of pictures. The pictures were of a clockmaker at work, Big Ben, cog-wheels and prints of pictures by Kandinsky (circles) and Van Gogh (sunflowers). The children were asked to bring clocks to add to the display: they brought alarm clocks, cuckoo clocks and a musical clock.

The children continued the work by making their own clock—a shadow clock. They set up goal posts and high-jump posts, or any straight structure that would cast a shadow in the playground. They went back to it every half-hour and chalked the shadow's position and length on the ground.

The work on shadow clocks led to work in groups and resulted in children experimenting with candle clocks, sand clocks, water clocks and pendulums. For example, the group working on candle clocks had a lighted taper and found it would burn steadily if it were out of a draught. They lit the taper and blew it out after fifteen minutes. Then they estimated how long it would burn for and, to test the accuracy of their estimations, they relit it and timed it again. They made up topic books to put their writing and drawings in, and made covers for these with

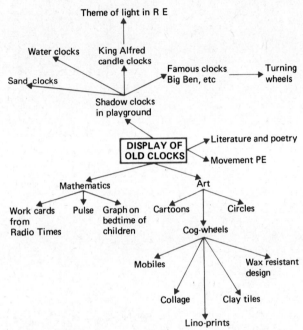

a wax-resistant design using cog-wheel shapes. The theme of light in RE stemmed from the work with candle clocks.

Looking at the workings of mechanical clocks led to work on turning wheels. The children investigated spinning wheels, water wheels, coal-mine cage wheels, potters' wheels, penny-farthing wheels, racing bicycle wheels, motorbike and car wheels, funfair wheels, wheels in an egg-beater and so on. They also imagined what it would be like in a world without wheels.

The child's day was illustrated by a series of cartoons showing the progression of time; prints of Kandinsky's work led to the children making tissue-paper designs of different circles stuck on to paper; cog-wheels led to a mobile with cog-wheel shapes in cardboard, to a lino-print design, a collage and to clay tiles where differing-sized cog-wheels had been pressed into the clay to make patterns.

In PE the children derived types of movement from mechanical toys and contrasted them with those derived from puppets. The teacher played records such as *The Clockmaker's Shop* and *The Fairy on the Clock.* The children improvised a sequence of movements on them singly and then in groups: for example, in one group one child set off the movement of other children like cog-wheels and the children cartwheeled round.

The teacher had made up a series of work cards from the *Radio Times* with questions aimed at finding out the length of the children's favourite programmes, and how much television they watched. A graph was made showing the bedtime of the children. Pulse beats were taken for three separate minutes and an average taken. The children then went out and skipped and took their pulse rates again. They also counted how many times they skipped in one minute. This led to a discussion on length of time and how it seemed to vary; for example, the children thought that a three-minute ride at the fair seemed a very short time.

Poems were written on clocks and time, and the teacher read them poems; for example, *Some Time,* by Eleanor Farjeon, and *School's Out,* by Hal Summers. The museum service yielded a record of Ted Hughes reading his poem *The Thought Fox,* which refers to time. The children collected references to time, such as time flies, and a stitch in time saves nine. The teacher read, as a follow-up to the candle clock, Hans Andersen's *Little Match Girl* and the children all had lighted candles on their desks to look into and imagine what could be seen there.

Lino-print of cog-wheels

Classroom activities

A sequence of events

Many young children of about five to six years of age have difficulty with the idea of a sequence of events. It is easy to check this by presenting them with a number of pictures showing a series of events during the day in getting up, break-fasting, play-time and so on. Can they put the pictures in order?

Infants of five to six often make a picture clock, showing what they do at various times of the day. This helps to develop the idea of a daytime sequence.

Other classroom activities suitable for very young children are:

Comparing things that move slowly with those that move quickly. Children can cut out pictures from magazines and mount them.

Making individual books with pictures showing those things that children do slowly and those things they do quickly.

Talking about yesterday, today and tomorrow in order to get these terms clear.

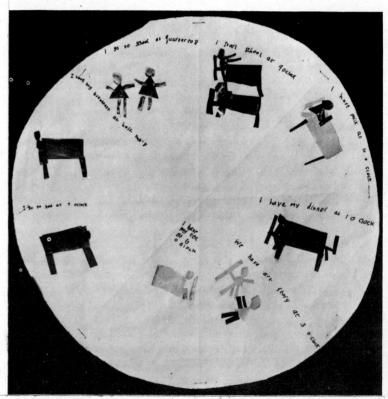

Picture clock

The duration of events

Measuring how long things take to happen is a fundamental activity that all children in the primary school come up against. Here are some suggestions of events to time with young children.

Timing:

How long it takes to walk down a corridor.

How long it takes to walk down a corridor balancing a book on one's head.

Songs.

Changing for PE.

Hopping, walking, running the length of the playground ; compare walking and running times.

Skipping over a given distance.

Skipping on the spot.

Washing, tying a shoelace, putting a coat on, combing hair and so on.

How long it takes to come to school on the bus.

A candle burning.

The number of things one can draw in a minute.

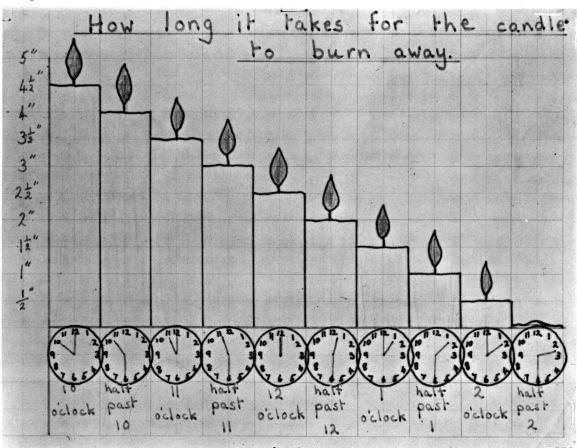

How long it takes for the candle to burn away.

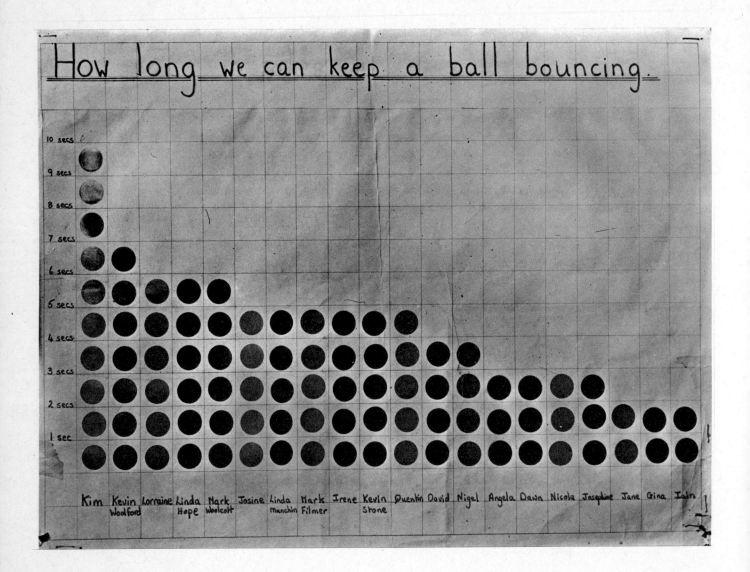

How long we can keep a ball bouncing.

6

A squeezy bottle emptying.

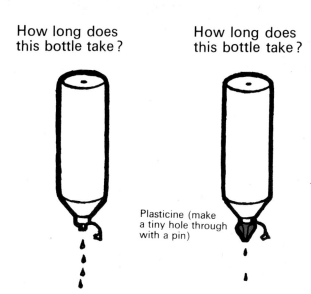

How long does this bottle take?

How long does this bottle take?

Plasticine (make a tiny hole through with a pin)

In all these activities children will be timing events that have a definite beginning and a definite ending; this results in their developing an appreciation of periods of time.

Estimation of time is also very important. Children can try to estimate how long an event will take and then compare their estimation with the time actually taken.

As children become older the events they time will increase in sophistication. They might time a toy train, clockwork toys, musical boxes, Dinky cars and marbles running down slopes. It is also interesting to make a chart showing how a day is spent or inspect the *Radio Times* to find the longest and shortest programmes and to compare them.

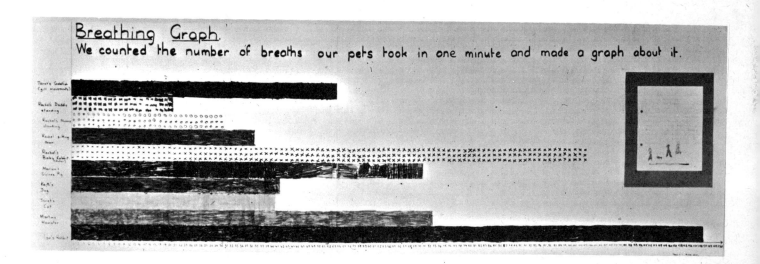

Breathing Graph.
We counted the number of breaths our pets took in one minute and made a graph about it.

Timers

What should be used to time events ? A clock with a second hand is best. There are, however, many other forms of timer that might be used. Try :

A metronome.

The pulse.

A rotating spot on a gramophone turntable (78 rev/min are best).

A flasher in an electric circuit.

A steadily dripping tap.

A ringing telephone bell.

An oscillating spring.

A car torch beacon.

Are a bouncing ball, skipping, breathing and counting out loud worth considering ?

The pulse

Children generally have difficulty in finding their pulses. It helps a number of them to be told exactly where to look. If the left hand is placed palm uppermost on the desk or table top, the pulse can be found with the index finger of the right hand. The thumb should not be used, because it has a pulse of its own. If the hand is palm uppermost, there is a bone, the radius, at the outside edge. A short distance from this there is a tendon. The pulse can be felt between the bone and the tendon.

Some children are able to show the actual movement of the pulse by balancing a drinking straw on a drawing pin and placing this on the pulse. The straw moves in time with the pulse ; the diagram on the right shows two ways in which it can be done.

What is the average pulse rate for a group of children ?

What is the pulse rate after running on the spot, running around the playground or after skipping ?

What timing aids are there outside the classroom ? There are :

Flashing pedestrian-crossing lights.

Police beacons.

Windscreen wipers.

Flashing neon lights.

Flashing Christmas tree lights.

Flashing lights on aeroplane wings.

Traffic lights (although the sequence is often irregular).

Wheels turning.

Windmills turning.

Natural movements, such as birds' wings beating or the wagging of a dog's tail, are, of course, irregular but still worth discussing.

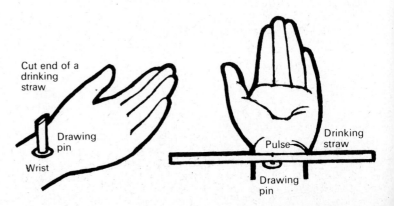

Inventing clocks

Much of the excitement of making a clock lies in devising it. It may be easy to present children with a ready-made recipe, but it is more difficult, but also more rewarding, to get the children to use materials and to think out a timer of their own.

Providing a wide variety of materials, ranging from candles to tin cans and a hammer and nails, will help. The following section of the book suggests the sorts of materials needed.

Give children plenty of time to think about what they want to make. A few will begin almost immediately, others will simply play with the material provided apparently without purpose. It is difficult to make a clock and their ideas will develop only slowly. Help and encourage, make suggestions to groups that are slow or not clear about what they are doing. Stimulate their thinking but try to let them solve their own problems, and do not ask too many questions—it may confuse them. In almost any situation there will be those children who need only a hint, or help with a piece of equipment, whilst there will be others who need much more definite suggestions and often even some specific instructions on what to do.

Shadow clocks

One of the common ways of making a shadow clock is to place an upright stick in the ground and mark in its shadow at fixed intervals of time.

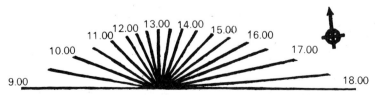

The properties of a shadow often perplex young children and it might be as well for them to carry out many of the shadow activities suggested in *Early experiences* before embarking on a shadow clock. Even sophisticated juniors find these fun.

The shadows cast by any subject, including the child himself, can be used to make a shadow clock. Try chalking in the shadow cast by the corner of the school building or by a net-ball post. Convert your results to a histogram.

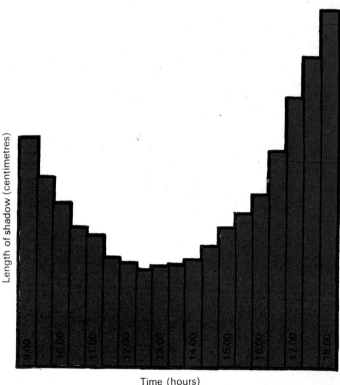

Histogram showing the relative length of a shadow during the day

Is the end of the shadow fuzzy?

Why does it change in length?

9

In 1967 one school in Bristol measured the length of the shadow cast at midday by a long pole. Because these children happened to work with some accuracy, they found that the time at which the shadow was shortest was not thirteen hours British Standard Time as they had expected. They soon realised that the time of the shortest shadow would be approximately ten minutes later than BST because Bristol is $2\frac{1}{2}°$ of longitude west of Greenwich (see Background information). However, the children still found variations for which they could not account. Using information from *Whitaker's Almanack,* a graph was drawn showing the times of sunrise and sunset and the time of shortest shadow calculated as half-way between these times. They set out their graph as follows.

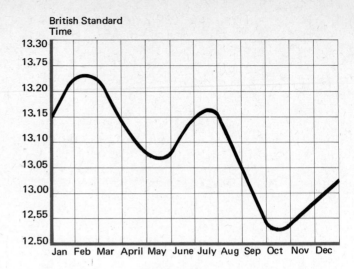

Variations in the time of shortest shadow throughout the year

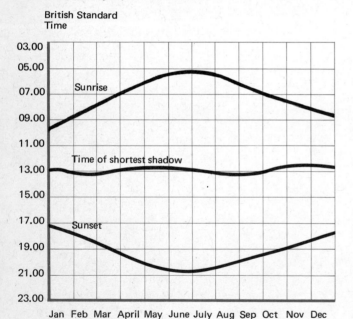

Time of sunrise, time of sunset and times of shortest shadow throughout the year

The children then drew a graph showing the time of shortest shadow on a much larger scale, obtaining a very interesting curve. (This links closely with the Equation of Time that is mentioned in Background information.)

Children working with a shadow stick

10

Following this work on shadow clocks using a long pole, a slim rod 1 dm in length was set up on a table and its shadow recorded on white paper whenever the weather allowed. These recordings were converted into histograms similar to the one shown earlier in the text.

Towards the end of March the children began to question the accuracy of their work, because they found that the ends of the shadow were now falling on a straight line running from east to west. Earlier in the year the ends of the shadows had traced a basin-like curve open to the north. The daily curves were examined closely, with a great deal of excitement and discussion, and the changes in shape during the year noticed. As the year progressed from the end of March, it was seen that the trace again became basin-shaped, but now open to the south. Maximum curvature came at about June 21st and then the curve gradually flattened. The changing pattern of the curve is shown below, though the sketches are not drawn to scale.

Spring, March 22nd

Summer, June 21st

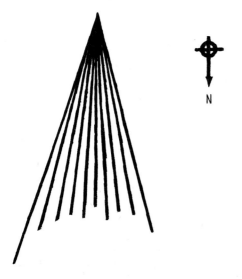

N

Winter, November 21st

A shadow calendar

If a school has a flagpole or other suitable large, free-standing structure it can be used to make a shadow calendar. The tip of the shadow should be marked at noon on the same day of the week through each week of the year. The marks should be painted in permanently, together with a record of the date. The area allowed for the task should be about as long from north to south as the height of the pole, and about as wide as half the height of the pole. The pattern formed by the shadow is intriguing and may well cause excitement among the children who are interested in this activity.

Sundials

Are there any sundials near the school? It is easy to make one.

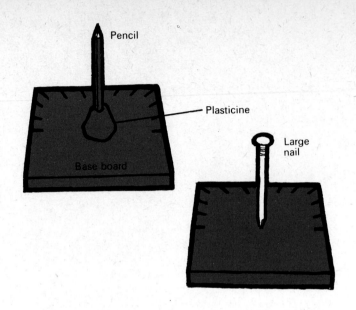

Pencil

Plasticine

Large nail

Base board

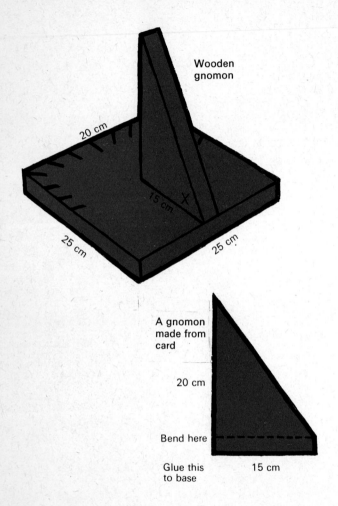

Wooden gnomon

20 cm

15 cm

X

25 cm

25 cm

A gnomon made from card

20 cm

Bend here

Glue this to base

15 cm

A bottle sundial

Point this sundial to the north.

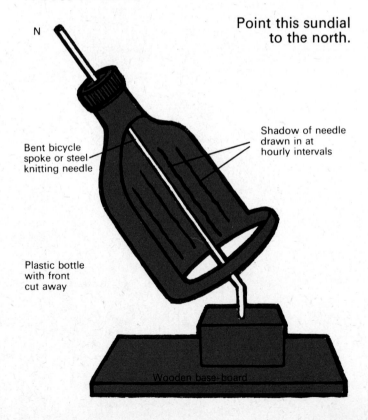

N

Bent bicycle spoke or steel knitting needle

Shadow of needle drawn in at hourly intervals

Plastic bottle with front cut away

Wooden base-board

The angle *X* should be equivalent to the latitude at which the school is situated. The gnomon is therefore parallel to the axis of the earth so that the sun appears to rotate round it and hence the shadow rotates at a uniform rate of 15° per hour. The approximate angle for Britain can be obtained by cutting out the gnomon to the measurements given in the diagram. Schools have improvised and tried out lots of other sundials.

Egyptian shadow clock
Model of a portable Egyptian shadow clock of a type built before the eighth century BC.

It was pointed towards the sun so that the shadow of the crossbar fell on the hour scale on its handle. The scale included five hour lines plus the noon line.

In the morning the shadow clock was held with the crossbar towards the east, then it was turned to the west for the afternoon.

Another sundial
Look up your latitude in an atlas.

Subtract it from 90°. This will give you angle *X*. Mark off the face into twelve angles of 15° each as shown. Fix in a needle or large nail.

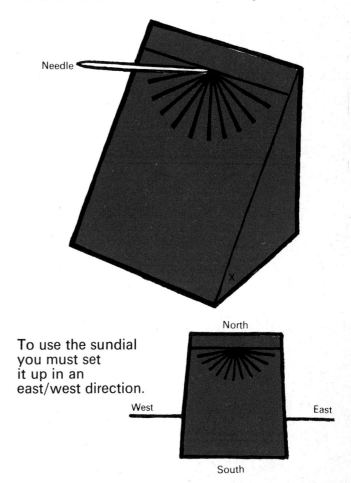

Needle

X

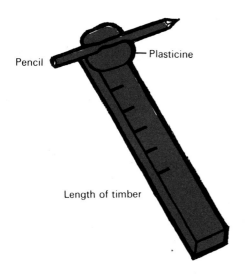

Pencil

Plasticine

Length of timber

To use the sundial you must set it up in an east/west direction.

North

West

East

South

Water clocks

Water clocks are easily improvised from yoghurt cartons, squeezy bottles, tin cans and other similar containers. A good large container is often useful, such as a plastic bucket or an old bath.

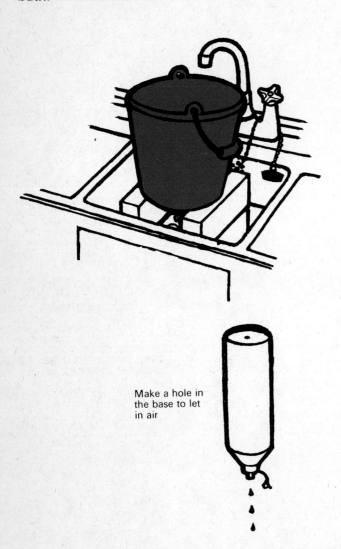

Make a hole in the base to let in air

The main variables to consider are the height of the water and the size of the aperture the water runs through.

Time the emptying of squeezy bottles with differing hole sizes. Make a graph of the time of emptying against the size of the aperture.

Some further problems:

Will a bottle with a 4-mm ($\frac{1}{8}$-in) hole empty twice as fast as one with a 2-mm ($\frac{1}{16}$-in) hole? This problem might be a nice lead into linear dimensions and area for many children.

How long does sand, water, soap solution and glycerine, or any other suitable material, take to run out of a water clock?

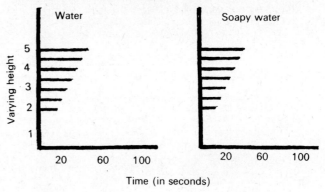

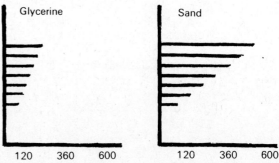

Add a weak soap solution (one per cent) to an already calibrated water clock. What effect does the detergent have on the emptying of the clock?

Try calibrating bottles with larger holes. Does the detergent have an effect if the holes are larger? Is a water clock sensitive to temperature? Try timing the emptying of a water clock using cold water then hot water.

A variety of water clocks

The degree of sophistication and the ingenuity used in making clocks can vary enormously. Here are a few suggested by schools.

A sinking water clock

The construction is shown in the diagram.

Plasticine

Plastic bowl with hole in base

Weight the bowl with Plasticine to stabilise it in the water.

Add washers.

Study the effect of the number of washers on rate of sinking.

Water alarm clock

The construction is shown in the diagram.

When the insulating tape is removed the water flows into the bottom bottle.

The float rises and makes contact across the wires, causing the bell to ring.

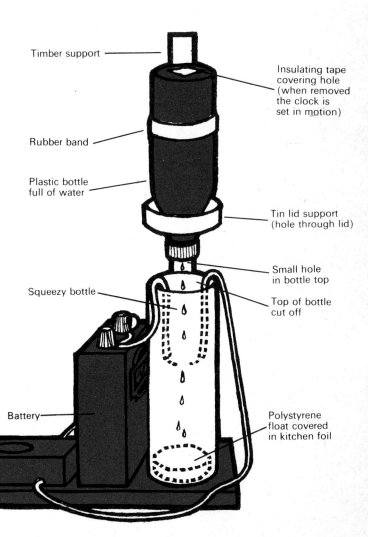

Timber support

Insulating tape covering hole (when removed the clock is set in motion)

Rubber band

Plastic bottle full of water

Tin lid support (hole through lid)

Small hole in bottle top

Squeezy bottle

Top of bottle cut off

Battery

Polystyrene float covered in kitchen foil

Electric bell

A Chinese water clock

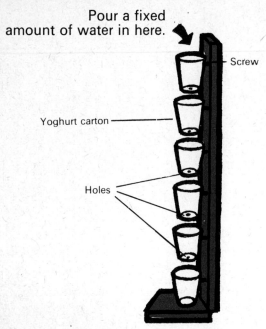

Pour a fixed amount of water in here.

Screw

Yoghurt carton

Holes

How long does the water take to reach the bottom carton?

Water clock with a float

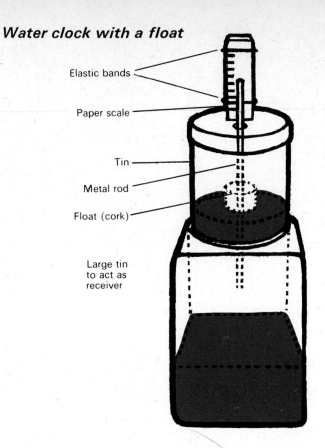

Elastic bands

Paper scale

Tin

Metal rod

Float (cork)

Large tin to act as receiver

Use a watch to calibrate the scale.

Why do the minute marks come closer together at the bottom of the scale?

Another water clock

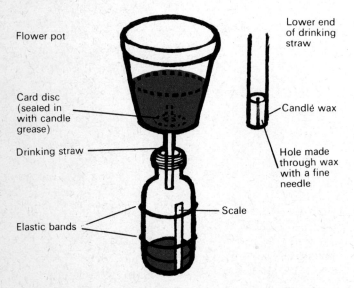

Flower pot

Card disc (sealed in with candle grease)

Drinking straw

Elastic bands

Scale

Lower end of drinking straw

Candle wax

Hole made through wax with a fine needle

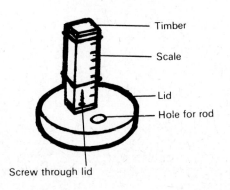

Timber

Scale

Lid

Hole for rod

Screw through lid

Water clock with screw clip

Adjust the screw clip
for a slow rate of drip.

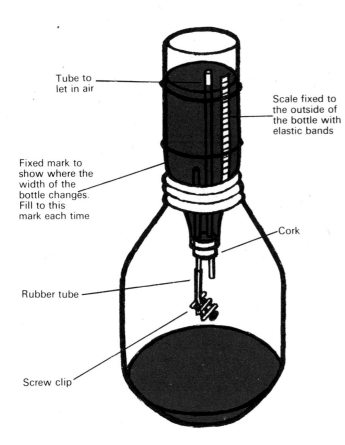

Tube to
let in air

Scale fixed to
the outside of
the bottle with
elastic bands

Fixed mark to
show where the
width of the
bottle changes.
Fill to this
mark each time

Cork

Rubber tube

Screw clip

Make sure the receiving jar is big enough to take
all the water without the water level reaching the
end of the air intake tube.

More water clocks

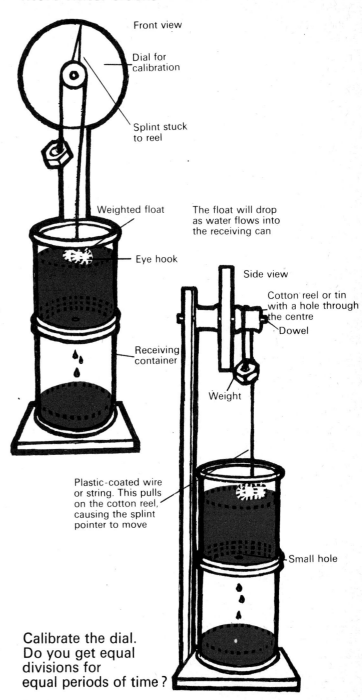

Front view

Dial for
calibration

Splint stuck
to reel

Weighted float

The float will drop
as water flows into
the receiving can

Eye hook

Side view

Cotton reel or tin
with a hole through
the centre

Dowel

Receiving
container

Weight

Plastic-coated wire
or string. This pulls
on the cotton reel,
causing the splint
pointer to move

Small hole

Calibrate the dial.
Do you get equal
divisions for
equal periods of time?

17

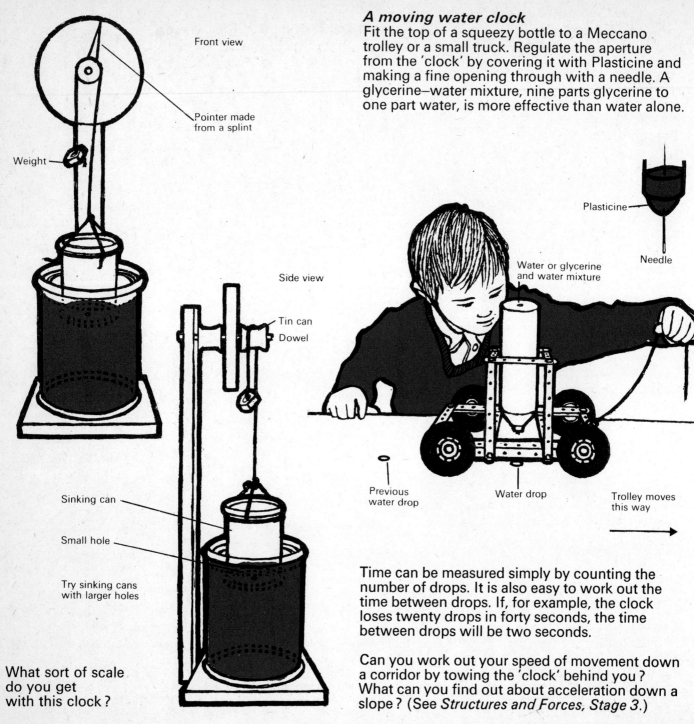

Front view

Pointer made from a splint

Weight

Side view

Tin can
Dowel

Sinking can

Small hole

Try sinking cans with larger holes

What sort of scale do you get with this clock?

A moving water clock

Fit the top of a squeezy bottle to a Meccano trolley or a small truck. Regulate the aperture from the 'clock' by covering it with Plasticine and making a fine opening through with a needle. A glycerine–water mixture, nine parts glycerine to one part water, is more effective than water alone.

Plasticine

Needle

Water or glycerine and water mixture

Previous water drop

Water drop

Trolley moves this way

Time can be measured simply by counting the number of drops. It is also easy to work out the time between drops. If, for example, the clock loses twenty drops in forty seconds, the time between drops will be two seconds.

Can you work out your speed of movement down a corridor by towing the 'clock' behind you? What can you find out about acceleration down a slope? (See *Structures and Forces, Stage 3*.)

18

Sand clocks

Sand clocks are fairly easy to make, but the sand must be dry and finely sifted. Here are two examples.

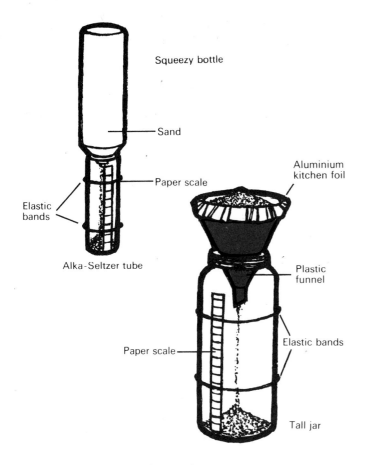

Make a collection of egg-timers borrowed from home.

How consistent is *each one* in time of emptying? Do all the egg-timers take the same time to empty? What extremes, in time of emptying, are there between egg-timers? What effect does this have on boiled eggs?

Have a look at the sand pulse-timer sometimes used by nurses. Have you got a telephone call timer?

Candle clocks

How many ways can children devise for calibrating a candle clock? Perhaps by:

Marking a control candle every fifteen or thirty minutes.

Measuring how much burns away in a given time.

Recording on a scale placed behind the candle.

Timing how long a given length of the candle takes to burn.

Be sure to take great care with burning candles. Put them on shelves which are too high for children to bend over them and keep them away from anything inflammable.

Try placing pins in a candle at given intervals and noting when they ping on a tin-lid base.

Let us call such intervals candle units.

How many candle units are there in a day?

How many candle units make up the school day?

Collect a variety of candles: kitchen candles, nightlights, wax tapers, inexpensive fancy candles, dinner candles and birthday candles. Make up a range of clocks.

One well-known firm of candle makers claims that its nightlights are designed to burn for eight hours. Can you devise a set of conditions under which to test such a claim?

Some simple, but ingenious, candle alarm clocks devised by children are shown on the next page.

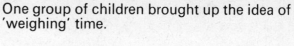

Taper

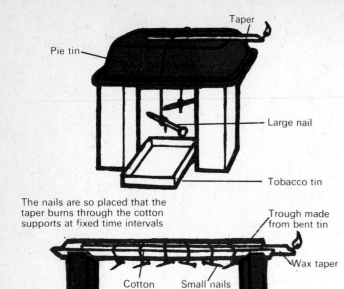

Pie tin

Large nail

Tobacco tin

The nails are so placed that the taper burns through the cotton supports at fixed time intervals

Trough made from bent tin

Wax taper

Cotton   Small nails

Timber support

Tin lid

One group of children brought up the idea of 'weighing' time.

As the nightlight shown in the apparatus below loses weight the pointer moves over the scale.

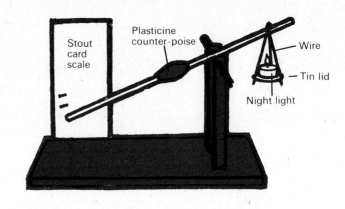

Stout card scale

Plasticine counter-poise

Wire

Tin lid

Night light

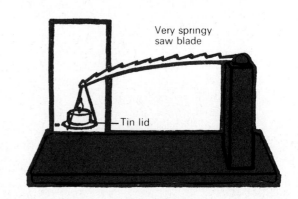

Very springy saw blade

Tin lid

Children with a candle alarm

Calibrate the scale as the candle loses weight. Try calibrating the clock in different parts of the room on successive days. Can you account for any discrepancies?

Mechanical clocks

'Why is a grandfather clock tall ?'

'When I take the back off my watch there's a little wheel that moves to and fro. What is it for ?'

A clock is an intricate piece of machinery, but the way it functions is relatively easy to understand.

There is usually a mechanism :

For driving the clock   *Falling weights or a spring.*

For regulating the clock   *A pendulum or hairspring.*

To link the driving device with the regulating mechanism   *An escapement mechanism.*

The hands are connected to the escapement mechanism. They move at a regulated speed over the calibrated dial.

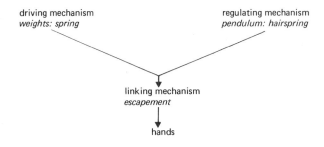

driving mechanism
weights: spring

regulating mechanism
pendulum: hairspring

linking mechanism
escapement

hands

Pendulums

What other pendulums can you think of ?
Set up a pendulum in school.

Play with the pendulum. Let it swing in wide and small arcs.

Do not forget to remove the eye-hooks before you close the door.

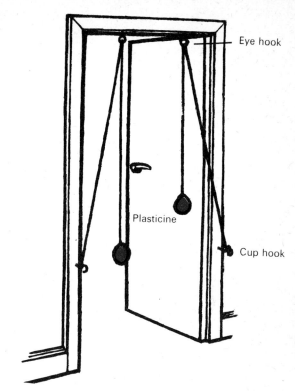

Eye hook

Plasticine

Cup hook

Try swinging a pendulum in a circle. Can you knock a skittle down ?

Swinging in a circle

Knocking down a skittle

Skittle

21

Pendulums

Try swinging two pendulums of *different lengths* at the same time and compare the swings.

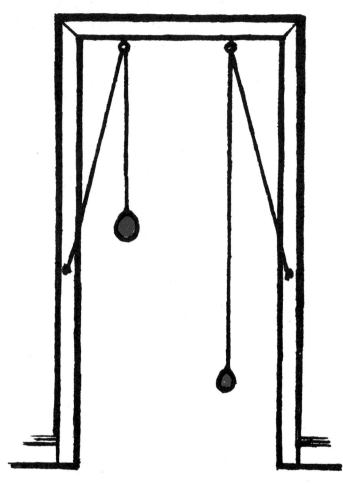

What do you notice?

What changes do you have to make to get the two pendulums to swing in time with one another?

Children will discover that the length of the pendulum is the critical factor in the time of each swing. When they have the two pendulums swinging together they could be encouraged to check whether they keep together for ten swings, twenty swings, thirty swings.

Try a stick pendulum.
Try the bob in varying positions.

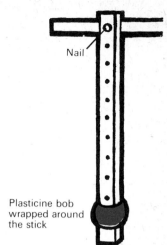

Nail

Plasticine bob wrapped around the stick

Variables and pendulums
There is no set pattern by which the variables involved in finding out about a pendulum may be investigated. For the sake of clarity each is considered separately.

a. Loss of motion
Start a pendulum bob swinging from a fixed mark, such as the end of an outstretched finger. Where does it return to?

Do you dare (with growing confidence) to start it from the end of your nose and keep your nose in position whilst the bob returns?

You'll need a steady hand!

Does weight affect loss of motion ? Compare heavy bobs with light ones. Does the motion die down more quickly with the lighter bob ?

A brick   A washer

Does size of the bob in relation to the weight have an effect on loss of motion ?

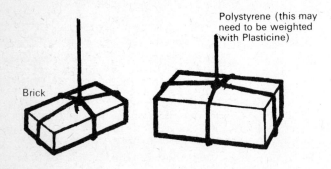

Brick

Polystyrene (this may need to be weighted with Plasticine)

Compare a brick with a block of polystyrene or compare a table tennis ball with a lump of Plasticine, of the same size.

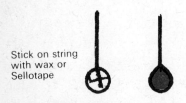

Stick on string with wax or Sellotape

b. Change of length
Children playing with the length of a pendulum will quickly discover that the shorter it is the quicker it will swing. Time the duration of the swing for different lengths of the pendulum. It would be best to time about twenty swings at each length.

Where do you measure ?

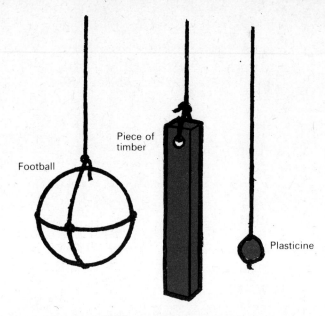

Piece of timber

Football

Plasticine

If the children are given pendulums like these illustrated to work with, they may try measuring the length of the pendulum to the centre of the bob.

Plot a graph of the time of about forty swings against length of the pendulum.

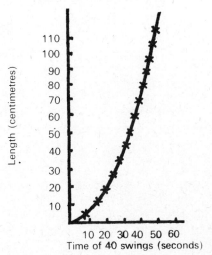

Find out, by interpolation from the graph, what length a pendulum which swings to and fro in exactly one second must be. This will then make a useful timer.

c. Change of weight
Is the weight of the bob going to have an effect? Try a number of pendulum bobs of different weights.

It is useful to have two pendulums swinging side by side.

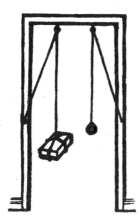

Will a pendulum with a heavy bob swing out further than a pendulum with a light bob?

It needs a lot of playing with bobs of different sizes and weights before children come to any conclusion about weight. Even so, it will be difficult for quite a number of children to accept that a change in the weight of the pendulum does not alter the time it takes for it to swing to and fro.

d. Amplitude
Does a wide swing of the pendulum take a longer time than a narrow swing? Time twenty wide swings of the pendulum. Time twenty narrow swings of the pendulum. Is there a difference?

Set a pendulum swinging in a loop to knock down targets.

Can you miss a matchbox on the outward journey but knock it down on the return journey?

How long does the bob take to move right round the loop?

Time twenty swings in a big circle and compare them with the time of twenty swings in a small circle.

Salt pendulums
These are fun to make and use. They make a variety of intriguing patterns. Make a hole in the base of a squeezy bottle and thread some plastic-coated wire through.

Tie it to a match-stick and suspend the squeezy bottle from a support.

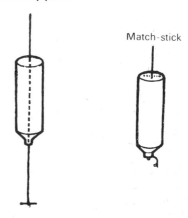

Match-stick

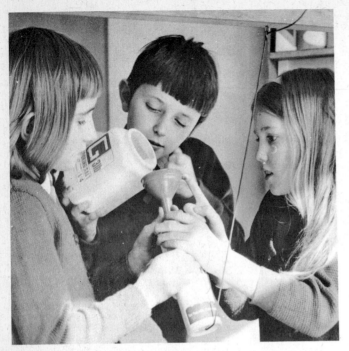

Putting in the salt

Salt pendulum in action

Put a cupful of salt into the bottle.

Salt

Set the salt pendulum swinging above a sheet of black sugar-paper.

Make sure that the squeezy bottle is *only just free* of the paper so that the salt doesn't scatter too much as it leaves the hole. What sort of patterns can you make?

Try colouring the salt by adding a pinch of dry powder paint and shaking the mixture well. Many schools have tried making permanent patterns.

This can be done by:

Dropping the salt on to a sheet covered with a thin layer of wallpaper paste.

Letting salt fall on to blueprint paper, exposing the paper to sunlight and then washing the paper in water.

Putting a thick salt *solution* in the bottle and letting drops that fall dry and crystallise out on paper.

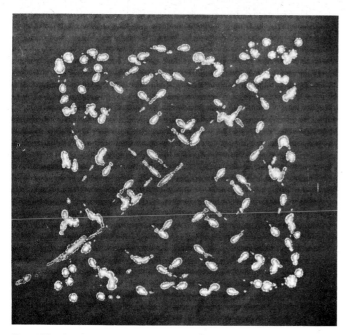

Crystallised drops

A salt pendulum trace

Fix some sheets of paper together and draw them along the floor beneath a pendulum swinging in an arc.

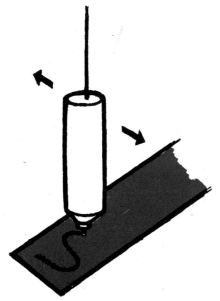

Salt pattern stuck with wallpaper paste

What does the trace tell you about the movement of the pendulum?

Where does the salt pile up highest?

What does this tell you?

Try swinging a salt pendulum back and forth over a line of yoghurt cartons.

Which carton holds most salt?

Which least?

What does this tell you?

Double suspensions
Patterns from a double suspension:

Try suspending a salt pendulum from two points.

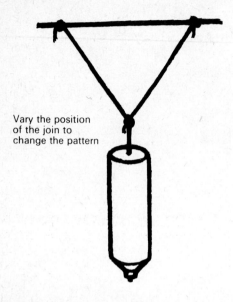

Vary the position of the join to change the pattern

Investigate a pendulum with a double suspension. What happens when you change the length of the strings? What happens when you change the distance between the strings?

What happens if you increase or decrease the size of the Plasticine bobs at the ends of the knitting needle?

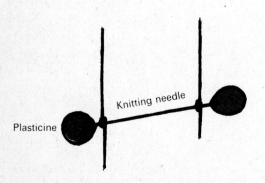

Plasticine

Knitting needle

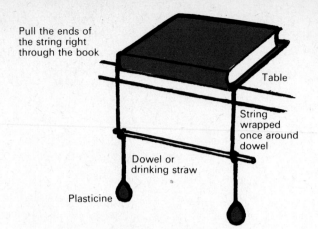

Pull the ends of the string right through the book

Table

String wrapped once around dowel

Dowel or drinking straw

Plasticine

Coupled pendulums
Set up two pendulums so that they are joined or coupled together, as shown above.

Hold one pendulum bob and set the other swinging.

Release your grip on the first pendulum. That is, set one bob moving while the other is held stationary, then release the second.

What happens?

Try raising and lowering the position of the coupling stick. What happens?

What happens if you:

Slant the coupling stick?

Change the weight of the bobs?

Replace the wooden coupling by one made of insulating tape?

The escapement mechanism
Clocks are usually driven by either a wound-up spring or a falling weight which unwinds from a drum. The release energy from these devices is controlled by the pendulum through the escapement mechanism. The continual release of energy keeps the pendulum swinging.

The best way to understand an escapement is from a working model.

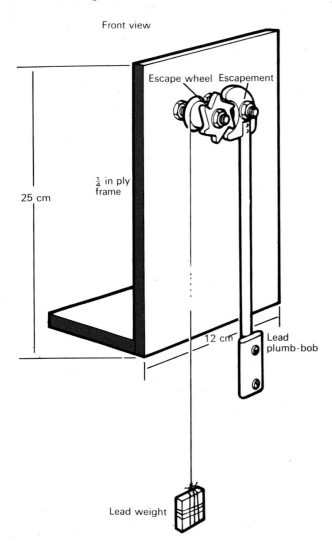

Front view

Escape wheel   Escapement

¼ in ply frame

25 cm

12 cm   Lead plumb-bob

Lead weight

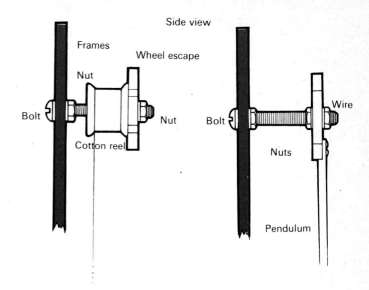

Side view

Frames

Wheel escape

Nut

Bolt

Nut

Cotton reel

Bolt

Wire

Nuts

Pendulum

Templates of the escape wheel and the escapement

The distance apart of the escape wheel and the escapement is very critical if you want to get your model working properly. If you want the model to tick seconds the pendulum must be 99·2 cm long. This is if the weight of the wooden rod is negligible compared with the weight of the bob. Perhaps it will be easier to move the bob up and down until it agrees with a watch.

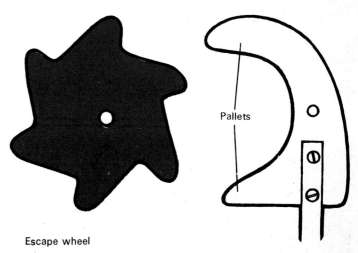

Escape wheel

Pallets

Escapement

Sky clocks

As the earth revolves on its axis the stars appear to spin in one direction and the earth in another. If children are shown how to locate the Plough and follow the pointers to find the Pole Star *Polaris* they will be able to see, when out in the evening, that the constellations appear to revolve around this Pole Star in an anti-clockwise direction.

The apparent spinning of the constellations around the Pole Star can be used to construct a star clock. This clock will differ from an ordinary clock in that its hands turn in an anticlockwise direction, *since this is the way the stars appear to turn,* and it has a twenty-four-hour face, *since the sky makes a complete turn in a day.*

There are several books that will give the principal stars for each month (for example, *Stars at a Glance*, George Phillip & Son Ltd, London). Work can begin from these.

If, for example, children look up in the book the position of the stars for midnight on March 22nd, they will find that the constellation of Cassiopeia is in association with the Plough as indicated below.

An imaginary line can be drawn between the Pole Star and Caph, one of the stars of the constellation of Cassiopeia, to represent the 'hour hand' of the clock. This, at midnight on March 22nd, would be pointing directly downward. Two hours later the hour hand position would be :

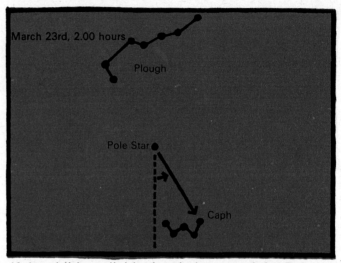

If the children divide the circle around the Pole Star into 360° they would find that the hour hand has moved through 30° in these two hours or one-twelfth of the circle. Another example is given below, where the time is now 22.00 hours (10 o'clock on March 22nd.)

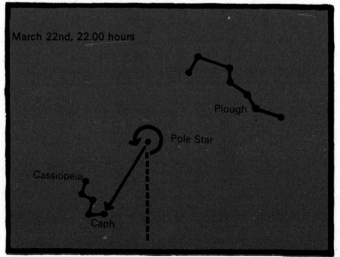

30

Children usually find it easier to understand such a clock by visualising its face as being split into quarters. It is then relatively easy to imagine one of these quarters divided into three parts, each of two hours' duration.

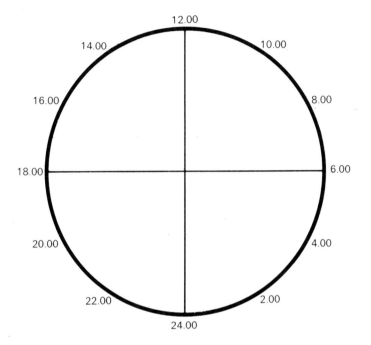

This clock is right for March 22nd but would be wrong on the other days of the year. This is because a complete rotation of the stars takes 23 h 56 min—a sidereal day—as opposed to the solar day of 24 hours (see 'Background information'). The stars thus appear to turn faster than the passing of an ordinary solar day and a star will be seen in the same position in the night sky four minutes earlier each evening or about two hours earlier each month. Therefore a correction of two hours must be made for each month or a half-hour for each week. The correction is added for time after March 22nd and subtracted for time before March 22nd.

The passage of time

There are many factors in the environment that change with time. The following are worth looking at with children.

Phases of the moon
Where does the moon rise and where does it set? A few individuals within a class might be interested enough to sketch the moon at the *same time* each evening in relation to the predominant features of the landscape. This will bring in not only its change in shape but also its change in position in the sky.

Preparing a set of cards with the landscape already drawn in will help.

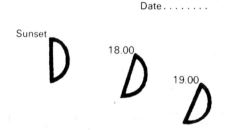

The phases of the moon are difficult to understand and a simple demonstration might help. Use a darkened classroom or the school stage and set up a filmstrip projector so that a beam of light shines across the room in front of the children.

A large white ball can then be moved in an arc through the beam of light and each child sees his own phases of the moon.

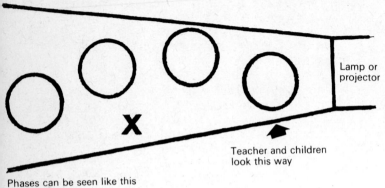

X

Teacher and children look this way

Lamp or projector

Phases can be seen like this

If the model moon is made to wane the lamp will have to be arranged on the opposite side to that shown in the diagram, but an individual standing at X can see the whole thing by continuing to move the model moon round until it goes out into the shadow again.

There are other interesting things to do concerning the moon:

What is the relationship between the moon and the calendar?
What sort of calendar do Semitic races use?

What is the relationship between the moon and the tides?

Collect photographs and examine the surface on both sides of the moon.

Look up the times of full moon in a diary and work out the times between moons. Check these against your own observations.

Day and night

With very young children observation of the sun at the beginning of the school day, at noon and at the end of the day is useful. They then have three fixed reference points to mark the passage of time.

Do not look directly at the sun.

A few schools with groups of eleven-year-olds have plotted the position of the sun through the day. Using a clinometer and plane table, readings of the sun's position in relation to prominent features of the landscape have been plotted through the months of the year.

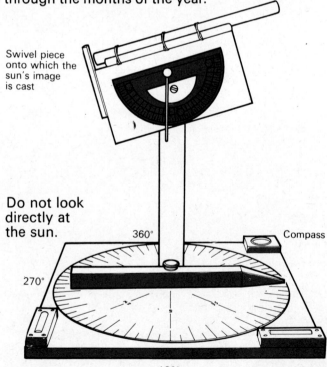

Swivel piece onto which the sun's image is cast

Do not look directly at the sun.

360°

270°

Compass

180°

The results were set out as shown in the chart below.

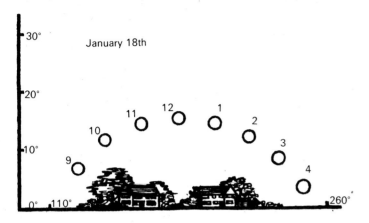

January 18th

Plotting a graph of the hours of darkness and light using data published in diaries can also be interesting.

The hours of sunshine on any one day are easily recorded. All that is needed is a large, deep tin with a firm-fitting lid. A *very small* hole should be made in the centre of the lid and the tin lined with blueprint or ferroprussiate paper. See diagram opposite.

Place the tin in a position free from shadow. Wash the blueprint paper at the end of the day in order to stabilise the trace.

Try graphing the number of hours of sunshine on each of the observation days.

Recipe for blueprint paper:

Ferric ammonium citrate (brown) and potassium ferricyanide are dissolved in water to make solutions: .

ferric ammonium citrate (brown)   187 g/1000 ml
potassium ferricyanide   137 g/1000 ml

Equal amounts of each solution are then mixed together. The resulting solution is painted on to non-glazed paper *in the dark*. This paper is then

allowed to dry and should be stored *away from light.* It is often useful to have the paper cut into rectangles that will fit the tin being used for sunshine recording. Such pieces of blueprint paper can then be stored ready for use in a biscuit tin or other suitable container.

The solution can also be made from green ferric ammonium citrate:

ferric ammonium citrate (green)   250 g/1000 ml
potassium ferricyanide   92 g/1000 ml

Alternatively ferroprussiate paper may be bought from:
Entwhistle, Phort & Co, Ltd, Tudor Industrial Estate, Ashton Street, Dunkinfield, Cheshire.

Very small hole

Blueprint paper

Reaction time

Among the events that children can time are those involving the speed of their own body's response to an external stimulus; that is, their reaction time. Begin by experiencing reaction time:

Drop a pebble and get your partner to catch it. Give no indication, of course, as to when the pebble is to be dropped.

Play snap. Count the number of tricks taken by individuals and draw up a score card indicating individual reaction times.

Then try some simple experiments:

Mark a long piece of card off into two centimetre intervals. Get a partner to stand with finger and thumb flanking the card as shown.

At what point does he catch the card when you let it fall?

Does his performance improve with practice?

Look up the section of the *Highway Code* that deals with reaction times and stopping distances.

An interesting group reaction time is passing a 'squeeze' around a circle. A large group of children (about fifteen) might stand in a circle facing outwards and holding hands. One child holds a stop-watch in his hand and, in this case, his neighbour holds his arm instead of his hand. The child with the stop-watch begins the activity by starting the stop-watch and *at the same time* uses his other hand to squeeze the hand of his neighbour. This child in turn squeezes his neighbour's hand and so the squeeze is passed around the circle until it reaches the child with the stop-watch. Once he feels his arm being squeezed he stops the stop-watch. The time is duly noted.

The children can then repeat this activity and will probably find that the time taken becomes shorter. With practice they find that the time becomes less and less until a minimum time is reached. Other groups from the class can repeat this experiment and the ensuing results compared.

Further ideas

Schools have found many other aspects of time that have been worth following. Here are some suggestions:

Group reaction time

Times at sea
Find out how sailors divide the day and night into *watches* and how each watch is divided into bells. (See 'Background information'.)

Dawn chorous
One school tape-recorded the dawn chorus and learned to identify the birds. Here are their results:

Times at which some of our birds started to sing

	Minutes before sunrise
Blackbird	45
Thrush	42
Robin	37
Crow	35
Wren	22
Starling	20
Great tit	19
Sparrow	18
Collared dove	17
Blue tit	12
Chaffinch and greenfinch	10

The seasons
Discuss the seasons as a means of telling what time of year it is and make up a frieze.

What I do in a day
Make a large chart illustrating the sorts of things that are done in one day. The cycle of a day or of a year can be interesting.

Collecting pictures
Collecting pictures of different types of clocks.

Tempo
Use the different tempos of clocks to make up a song or a dance.

Time charts
Make a chart of time through the ages. Some schools made collections of objects to illustrate their time chart. For example, Roman pottery, models of knights in armour, old bottles, bed-warmers, an old travelling clock and other objects have featured in displays.

Background information

Units of time

The day
And God called the light day, and the darkness he called night. And the evening and the morning were the first day. (Genesis i. 5)

The day must have been the simplest and most striking unit of time for primitive man. Most languages do not have a term for day and night together, which indicates that the realisation that they were parts of a single unit probably came at a late date in man's history. The period of twenty-four hours is denoted in most languages by the term that denotes the light part, ie day.

Some people believe that Stonehenge is a giant calendar. The position of the stones shows the position of sunrise and sunset and of moonrise and moonset in the summer and in the winter. Professor Gerald Hawkins sets out his theories in his book *Stonehenge Decoded*

The counting of days by using the sun is rare. The Comanche Indians of the American continent used this method, and an Indian hieroglyph from the northern shores of Lake Superior indicates the duration of a three-day journey by three circles, representing three suns. Most peoples counted from the nights—for example, the Arabs used the phrases 'in three nights' and 'on the first night of Ramadan'. The Pawnees used to cut notches in a stick to mark the passage of the nights and denoted the night by the word 'sleep' or 'sleeping time'. Thus journeys took so many 'sleeps'. This method of counting in 'sleeps' is also used by the aborigines of Central Australia.

Indication of time within the day was probably by reference to the sun. There is evidence that a number of primitive peoples indicate a time by pointing to the position that the sun will occupy in the sky; some peoples used the length of shadows. A very rich terminology is often apparent among many primitive peoples. The Kiowa Indians have dawn (literally: 'first light'), sunrise (literally: 'the-sun-has-come-up'), morning (literally: 'full day'), noon, early afternoon until about three o'clock, late afternoon and evening (literally: 'first darkness').

The Eskimos of Greenland were the only people known to reckon time by the ebb and flow of the tides. They were also very accurate observers of the heavens and could indicate time from the star Vega, or from the Pleiades.

Timekeeping is thus based on a natural phenomenon, the rotation of the earth, giving the interval of one day. If sunrise and sunset are chosen as the limit to the day these must change every day and the days will vary in length. Subdivision of the day into twenty-four hours has come down from remotest ages. In antiquity the hour was a twelfth part of the whole time of daylight. This duodecimal system was switched also to the night, which had commonly been divided into four watches, a practice which came from military life. It was probably with the growth of sophistication in society, such as in Rome under the Caesars, that it became necessary to time events in the night. As the length of the day and the night varied with the time of year, so the hour also varied when the period was divided into equal parts. This varying hour prevailed almost until the end of the Middle Ages in Europe and in Japan until the nineteenth century.

The modern hour has been in general use since the fourteenth century, when striking clocks came into use. It is an artificial unit and the day could equally well be divided into a number of units other than twenty-four.

Solar time
If we are to understand how the hour as we know it is determined, we must consider the earth in orbit round the sun. This orbit is slightly elliptical and as a consequence the earth's distance from the sun varies. Pulled in this elliptical orbit by the gravitational attraction of the sun, the earth's velocity is greater in January, when it is near the sun, than it is in July, when it is further away. In addition one must remember that the earth's axis is inclined and because of this the sun's apparent movement relative to the equator is not uniform.

Thus the *apparent solar day*, that is the time from noon to noon, will vary in length through the year. For example, because the velocity of the earth in January is greater than it is in July, the July day is about fifteen seconds longer when measured by apparent solar time. For everyday use an *average* day is calculated and divided into twenty-four equal hours. Such time is spoken of as *mean solar time* (often called *local* time).

The difference between mean solar time and apparent solar time (as measured by a sundial) is spoken of as the 'equation of time'. The word equation is here used in its old meaning of correction. These two sorts of time chase one another through the year, one first being ahead of and then behind the other, with the greatest difference (of about sixteen minutes) occurring in November.

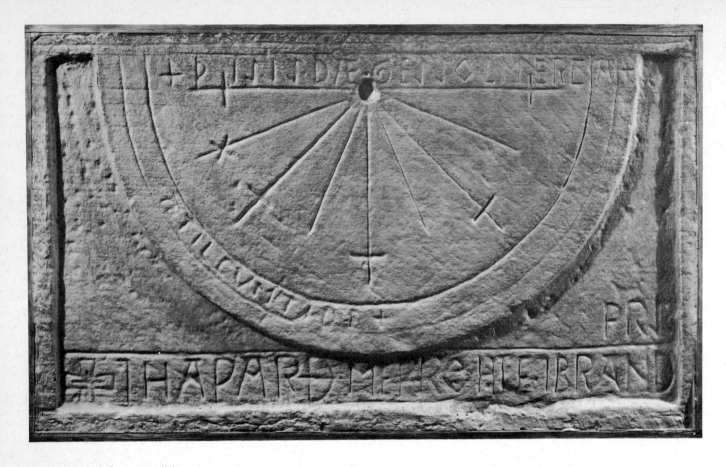

Plaster cast of a Saxon sundial

Sidereal time

Not all nations begin the day in the same period. Among the ancient Egyptians and the Europeans the beginning of the day has been placed at midnight, with the morning hours from midnight to noon and the evening hours from noon to midnight. Astronomers, however, from the time of Ptolemy have taken an hour of constant length and regard the day as commencing at noon.

The astronomers use the stars to tell their time and they do this by measuring the time the earth takes to complete one rotation on its axis with respect to a fixed star. Such a time is constant in length and can be very accurately measured (see Greenwich, page 50). The astronomers' day is

termed a *sidereal day* (Latin, *sidus*, a star), and measures *sidereal time.*

Sidereal time allows a very accurate measurement of the earth's rotation. When the earth has rotated through 360° it must turn about 1° more (because it is also circling the sun) in order to gain the same relative position that it had to the sun twenty-four hours previously. Thus astronomers use a fixed star instead of the sun, because the great distance away of such a star makes the movement of the earth in its orbit of little importance.

A sidereal day is about four minutes shorter than

a mean solar day. These minutes accumulate from day to day and the ordering of civil life by such a system would be impracticable. Man lives by the sun and orders his life by mean solar time. Sidereal time is left to the astronomers.

Dividing the day
The civil day begins at midnight. The first twelve hours are designated am (Latin, *ante meridan*, before noon), the next twelve hours are designated pm (Latin, *post meridian*, after noon). The use of the twenty-four-hour clock is now becoming more common.

Clock (am and pm)	Clock (24 hour)
6.00 am	06.00
12.00 noon	12.00
3.15 pm	15.15
6.30 pm	18.30
12.00 midnight	24.00

British and European time
During World War I Daylight Saving Time was tried in Great Britain and the USA An extra hour of daylight was 'gained' by advancing the clock one hour ahead of Greenwich Mean Time (page 49) during summer, thus allowing people to work longer in agriculture. In World War II Double Summer Time was introduced in which timekeepers were set two hours ahead of GMT.

After World War II Britain adopted British Summer Time during the summer months, in which the clocks were set one hour ahead of GMT.Since February 18th, 1968, timekeepers have been set permanently one hour ahead of GMT thus bringing Great Britain into line with Central European Time. It was believed that this should result in less strain on power consumption at the end of the day because shops and offices would be later in switching on their power supplies. The experiment was stopped at the end of 1971.

The week
The week, like the hour, is a unit which is artificial and not dependent on celestial motions: it is a period of seven days which has been used

Days of the week

Latin	French
Dies Solis (Sun's day)	dimanche
Dies Lunae (Moon's day)	lundi
Dies Martis (Mars' day—god of war)	mardi
Dies Mercurii (Mercury's day— messenger of the gods)	mercredi
Dies Jovis (Jove's or Jupiter's day— ruler of the gods)	jeudi
Dies Veneris (Venus's day—goddess of love)	vendredi
Dies Saturni (Saturn's day—god of agriculture)	samedi

Saxon	English
Sun's day	Sunday
Moon's day	Monday
Tiw's day (Norse god of war)	Tuesday
Woden's day (Norse god of storms)	Wednesday
Thor's day (Norse god of thunder)	Thursday
Frigg's day (wife of Odin)	Friday
Sater's day (Saturn—Roman god of agriculture)	Saturday

In Eastern countries for a very long time and which was introduced to Rome in the time of Theodosius (c. AD 379–95).

The English names for the days of the week come from the Saxon. The Saxons followed the seven-day week of the Eastern nations and substituted the names of their own gods for those of the Greek deities. It is interesting to note that the French names for the days of the week are derived directly from the Latin ones.

The month
The revolution of the moon about the earth takes a period of approximately twenty-nine and a half days. This period of time is a lunar month. In its movement the moon changes position, both in relation to the earth and to the sun.

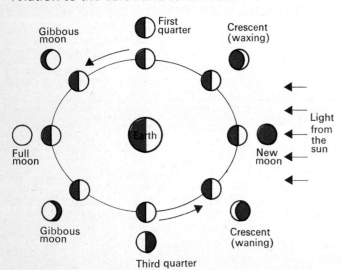

The outer ring of sketches shows the moon as it appears in the sky

As the diagram shows, when the moon is directly between the earth and the sun the side turned towards the earth is in shadow; it receives no light from the sun, is therefore unable to reflect light and we cannot see it from earth: it is the dark of the moon. But when the positions of earth and moon are reversed the moon receives and reflects light from the sun, and so we say there is a full moon. As the moon's surface facing the sun gets larger it reflects more and more light.

It is said to be waxing. As the reflecting surface gets smaller it reflects less and less light and it is said to be waning.

Twelve lunations form a period of 354 days which differs only by about eleven and a quarter days from the solar year. The year has become divided by convention into months; these are quite independent of the moon and keep as reminders of their origin only the name and a length approximating to that of the moon's revolution. This has happened because the moon, unlike the sun and the seasons, has no great effect on our daily lives. Among some peoples, however, the moon was often the only convenient measure of the duration of time and such peoples have judged their year by the moon.

The ancient Egyptians had a year of twelve months, each of thirty days, with five supplementary days added at the end of the year. By this method a quarter of a day was lost every year. This year is called *vague* because with the passage of time the lost quarter-days accumulate and the year starts earlier and earlier. Thus it commences sometimes at one season of the year and sometimes at another. The Muslim calendar still wanders in this way. The government of Israel uses the ancient Jewish calendar, which, like that of other Semitic races, is based on the moon. The year has twelve months, each of twenty-nine or thirty days, with the insertion of a thirteenth month seven times during every nineteen-year period.

The division of the year into months based on the Gregorian calendar is used by many countries. This is discussed in the next section.

The year
The natural year is conditioned by the passage of the earth around the sun, which takes 365 days 5 h 48 mins 46 s of mean solar time. Such an odd length of time has always caused trouble; it would have been more convenient had nature presented us with a whole number of days for reckoning.

There are two main problems. First, this odd length of time must be distributed in some way among the twelve months. Second, a means must be found of always beginning the year at approximately the same distance in time from the solstices or equinoxes. This is necessary in order to fit the seasons to the same time of year every year; otherwise the year would become *vague* like that of the Ancient Egyptians (see 'The month'). Obviously, since 365 is not divisible by twelve, each month cannot be the same length. In addition the odd 5 h 48 min 46 s must be accounted for.

Our civil calendar is adapted from that of the Romans. Originally the Roman calendar began with March, a clue to this being retained in our present calendar with the names. September, October, November and December follow the Latin numerals for the seventh, eighth, ninth and tenth months.

The Julian calendar
When Julius Caesar took over the administration of the Roman Empire he inherited a system which had been thrown into considerable confusion by the wiles of Roman officials, who had for personal gain changed the length of months in order to complete their own pet schemes. He called the Greek astronomer Sosigenes from Alexandria to help to put the calendar in order. Three hundred and sixty-five days were assigned to each year with every fourth or leap year having 366 days. This, of course, assumes a year of 365 $\frac{1}{4}$ days, longer than the solar time of 365 days 5 h 48 min 46 s by some 11 min 14 s.

The Julian calendar was inaugurated on January 1st, 45 BC (BC, 'before Christ', or sometimes AC, *ante Christum*). It began by being very neat and tidy. All the odd-numbered months, ie January, March, May, July, September and November had thirty-one days and all the others had thirty, except February, which had twenty-nine days. In a leap year February should have thirty days.

This tidy state of affairs was interrupted by

Augustus Caesar. July had been named after Julius Caesar and Augustus decided that he too would have a month to call his own. Hence arose our present month of August. Unfortunately this month, being the eighth month and therefore even numbered, had only thirty days. Augustus could not let Julius's month have more days than his and therefore Augustus took one day from February and added it to August. A number of thirty-one-day months now followed one another. Some swopping of days occurred to compensate for this and we end up with the situation given in the rhyme:

> Thirty days hath September,
> April, June and November,
> All the rest have thirty-one,
> Excepting February alone,
> Which hath but twenty-eight days clear,
> And twenty-nine in each leap year.

As mentioned earlier, there was a discrepancy of 11 minutes 14 seconds between the length of the year based on the Julian calendar and the length of the natural year.

The Gregorian calendar
In 1582 Pope Gregory XIII decided to reform the calendar, for the equinox which fell on March 25th when the Julian calendar was introduced now fell on March 11th. He ordered ten days to be suppressed from the calendar and brought in a new leap year rule to stabilise the calendar. Under the Julian calendar an error of three days occurs in every 400 years. Pope Gregory ordered that all years divisible by four should be leap years, except the centurial years (eg 1800, 1900). These only become leap years when the number is divisible by four after the two zeros are removed. Thus the centurial years 2000 and 2400 will be leap years.

The Gregorian calendar was introduced in England by Act of Parliament as late as 1752. Eleven days were suppressed after September 2nd, 1752. This led to rioting among certain sections of the population who, not understanding the new law, ran wild, crying 'Give us back our eleven days.'

The world calendar

In order to simplify events it has been suggested that a world calendar be set up. This would ensure that an event such as a birthday, for example, occurred on the same day of the week no matter what the year. It would also render the reprinting of the calendar unnecessary.

In this proposed calendar the months of January, April, July and October would have thirty-one days. The other months would have thirty. This would make a total of 364 days. The 365th day, called Worldsday, placed at the end of December, would be a universal holiday. In leap years an extra day would be added at the end of June.

It will be noted that the year, under this scheme, runs in four quarters beginning at the first of January. Each quarter begins on a Sunday and ends on a Saturday.

The World Calendar

January	February	March
S M T W T F S	S M T W T F S	S M T W T F S
1 2 3 4 5 6 7	1 2 3 4	1 2
8 9 10 11 12 13 14	5 6 7 8 9 10 11	3 4 5 6 7 8 9
15 16 17 18 19 20 21	12 13 14 15 16 17 18	10 11 12 13 14 15 16
22 23 24 25 26 27 28	19 20 21 22 23 24 25	17 18 19 20 21 22 23
29 30 31	26 27 28 29 30	24 25 26 27 28 29 30

April	May	June
S M T W T F S	S M T W T F S	S M T W T F S
1 2 3 4 5 6 7	1 2 3 4	1 2
8 9 10 11 12 13 14	5 6 7 8 9 10 11	3 4 5 6 7 8 9
15 16 17 18 19 20 21	12 13 14 15 16 17 18	10 11 12 13 14 15 16
22 23 24 25 26 27 28	19 20 21 22 23 24 25	17 18 19 20 21 22 23
29 30 31	26 27 28 29 30	24 25 26 27 28 29 30 [L]

July	August	September
S M T W T F S	S M T W T F S	S M T W T F S
1 2 3 4 5 6 7	1 2 3 4	1 2
8 9 10 11 12 13 14	5 6 7 8 9 10 11	3 4 5 6 7 8 9
15 16 17 18 19 20 21	12 13 14 15 16 17 18	10 11 12 13 14 15 16
22 23 24 25 26 27 28	19 20 21 22 23 24 25	17 18 19 20 21 22 23
29 30 31	26 27 28 29 30	24 25 26 27 28 29 30

October	November	December
S M T W T F S	S M T W T F S	S M T W T F S
1 2 3 4 5 6 7	1 2 3 4	1 2
8 9 10 11 12 13 14	5 6 7 8 9 10 11	3 4 5 6 7 8 9
15 16 17 18 19 20 21	12 13 14 15 16 17 18	10 11 12 13 14 15 16
22 23 24 25 26 27 28	19 20 21 22 23 24 25	17 18 19 20 21 22 23
29 30 31	26 27 28 29 30	24 25 26 27 28 29 30 [W]

The months of the year

January	Named after the double-faced Roman god Janus, who looks into both past and future
February	Named after Februa, a Roman festival of purification
March	Named after Mars, the Roman god of war
April	Derivation uncertain
May	Named after Maia, the Roman goddess of growth
June	Derivation uncertain
July	Named after Julius Caesar
August	Named after Augustus Caesar
September	Named after Latin *septem* (seven)
October	Named after Latin *octo* (eight)
November	Named after Latin *novem* (nine)
December	Named after Latin *decem* (ten)

Light years

A light year is the distance that light travels in one year, hence the light year is a measure of distance and not of time. Since the velocity of light is approximately 300 000 000 m/s, it is a simple matter to work out the distance traversed in one year. It is 300 000 000 × 60 (seconds) × 60 (minutes) × 24 (hours) × 365 (days) and equals 9 460 800 000 000 km.

The star Sirius in the constellation Canis Major is 8·7 light years away. Light from Sirius will take approximately 8·7 years to reach the earth. Its distance from the earth is therefore equal to 9 460 800 000 000 × 8·7, which comes to 82 308 960 000 000 km.

Time measurement

Until recently the passage of time could be measured only by considering the regular, or approximately regular, motion of a body. It might be the water or sand in a *clepsydra*, or water clock (Greek—'water thief'), the shadow cast by the gnomon of a sundial or the rotating wheel found in most modern clocks. The more regular the motion in a timepiece or clock is, the more accurate that clock would be. The history of clocks has been the history of attempts to make such motion perfectly uniform.

Early clocks

Man's use of the sun and other celestial bodies for measuring time has already been mentioned. Man's observations in this field would undoubtedly have led to the noting and use of shadows for telling the time; the Babylonians and Egyptians certainly used shadow clocks.

Water clocks or *clepsydrae* were used by the Egyptians and are amongst the earliest known timing devices to bear time-scales. These vessels were in the shape of a large bowl with markings on its inner surface which became exposed as the water ran out, usually through a small hole near the base. *Clepsydrae* became more sophisticated as the centuries passed and were often coupled with mechanisms which rang bells or beat on drums, or caused some form of movement of figures or 'jacks' as they are called.

The Saxons used both sundials and water clocks and some of these have survived to the present time. The water clock consisted of a bowl with a hole at its base. This was placed in water and after a fixed period of time sank, thus giving a unit of measurement. It is known that the Saxons divided their day—that is, the daylight hours—into four parts or 'tides'; the terms 'noontide' and 'eventide' are still in use. Asser, the biographer of King Alfred, has recorded that the king made use of candles as timekeepers. Each candle was divided into twelve divisions and burned away in four hours. The candle was protected from draughts and thus allowed to burn at a consistent rate by being placed in a wooden lantern with windows made of thin horn.

Sundials have persisted until the present time. 'Scratch' dials, so called because their markings are engraved on the actual stone, are still to be found on churches and may date from the twelfth century.

The modern garden sundial has a gnomon or central rod which points to either the true North or to the South Pole. It is usually triangular in shape and is so constructed as to present an angle with the horizontal equal to the latitude where the sundial is located so that its edge, that is the effective gnomon, is parallel to the axis of the earth. For London this is $51\frac{1}{2}°$.

Sand clocks, in which sand passes from one vessel to another, appeared during the Middle Ages.

They have been used for timing sermons, as well as eggs, and for timing watches on board ship.

One very important use of sand-glasses was for estimating speed on ships.

Cast of Egyptian water clock

Sand glasses 1720

Speed at sea

An early method of estimating the speed of a ship at sea had been to use as the measure of time, the time taken to say a paternoster. A piece of wood (hence the term log) was dropped overboard, a sailor then walked towards the stern saying his paternoster and keeping abreast of the 'log', the distance he had gone by the time he had completed his prayer was, of course, the distance the ship had gone in that rather unreliable unit of time—'the time taken to say a paternoster'.

Later a sand-glass replaced the paternoster and later still the hand-log in combination with a sand-glass was used.

The hand-log was a triangular piece of wood attached to the log line marked off by 'knots' (which were in fact knots in the thin rope). The log was dropped overboard from the stern of the ship while the line ran out from a rotating reel held above his head by a sailor. The officer of the watch turned the sand-glass when he felt the zero knot pass through his hand and he grabbed the line again when the sand ran out; the number of knots run out in the prescribed time gave the speed of the ship in *knots* (nautical miles/hour = 1,853 m/h). The sharp jolt as the line was caught pulled the peg out of the log so that the log now floated flat and was easily hauled in. In order to read off the number of knots run out easily in the dark every fifth knot was replaced by a piece of leather marked in a recognisable way ; for example, the tenth knot had a piece of leather with a round hole cut in it.

The interest in this account lies in the words log and knot. The speed of the ship was estimated at the end of each four-hour watch and entered in the log-book, which is, of course, a term now in general use and often abbreviated as the log.

The nautical mile is the mean length of one minute of arc on the earth's surface and the unit that must be used in navigation whatever happens to SI units ! The metre was originally designed to be one ten-millionth of the earth's quantrantal distance and therefore 10×10^6 m $= 1 \times 60 \times 90$ nautical miles, but the estimation of the mean distance from the pole to the equator made by Lacaille and Cassini in 1739, based on the distance of Dunkirk from Barcelona, has since been found to be inaccurate.

An interesting exercise is to find the distance between knots for a given sand-glass and to discuss the relative advantages and disadvantages of using a short timer (eg thirty seconds) and a long timer (eg two minutes).

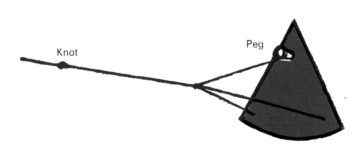

Knot   Peg

Mechanical clocks
The mechanical striking clocks are the only timekeeping instruments that should really be called a clock. The name comes from the Middle English form *clokke* or *clok* which means bell. The first mechanical clocks had no hands. They struck a bell at each hour, telling the time only in hours.

In mechanical clocks there are three main parts :

A driving mechanism, which provides the energy to drive the clock, and which may be falling weights, a wound-up spring or an electric motor.

A regulating mechanism, which ensures the clock keeps uniform time and which may be a pendulum or a balance spring.

A linking mechanism (the escapement), which links the driving mechanism with the regulating mechanism and breaks the energy of the driving mechanism so that it is released slowly and evenly.

The hands of the clock are connected to the escapement.

The first mechanical clocks date from the fourteenth century. They were, in the main, public clocks striking the hours for the populace at large. They were very big and heavy and were usually made by a blacksmith. These clocks were driven by falling weights.

The regulating mechanism was a *foliot balance*, a heavy bar pivoted near the centre which rotated first in one direction and then in another and was driven by a toothed wheel which was in turn harnessed to the falling weights.

The accuracy of clocks regulated by a foliot balance was not very great and consequently they were fitted with just the hour hand. It was only with the introduction of the pendulum in the seventeenth century and the resultant accuracy in timekeeping that minute hands came into widespread use.

The pendulum
Galileo (page 52) is credited with noticing that the time of swing of a pendulum is independent of the amplitude or width of its swing. If such a motion, with a defiinte period of swing, could be harnessed to a clock it could be used as a regulating device. This was carried out by the Dutch scientist Christian Huygens (page 54).

Its use quickly spread and many old clocks employing a foliot balance were adapted to take a pendulum.

What are the properties of a pendulum which make it so useful? First, as already stated, its time of swing will be independent of the size or amplitude of its swing (within a reasonable arc of about 6°). Second, the size of the plumb-bob, again within reason, will have no effect on the time of swing. The factor that does affect the swing of a pendulum is its length. The period of swing of a pendulum varies as the square root of the distance from the point of suspension to the centre of gravity of the plumb-bob. That is to say, if the length is increased four-fold this doubles its time of swing, or, a quarter the length will take half the time period to complete its swing.

The pendulum does have a drawback in that if it is metallic its length will change perceptibly with changing temperature. Its length will increase as the temperature rises, and decrease with a temperature drop. Various temperature-compensating devices have been invented and tried through the centuries since its use as a regulator was adopted. Invar, a nickel–iron alloy, is often used nowadays. It makes hardly any change in length for an alteration in temperature.

The escapement mechanism

In clocks and watches a wheel is made to rotate regularly backwards and forwards and its rotation is coupled to a system which moves the hands on the clock or watch face. The passage of time is thus recorded. The speed of rotation of this wheel is governed in clocks by the pendulum through the *escapement mechanism.* That is to say, the wheel has teeth upon its rim which lock into a mechanism called the 'escapement' that releases the teeth one at a time. This means that the wheel moves steadily, at a regulated pace. The wheel itself is called the escape wheel.

A timekeeper must have an escape wheel, an escapement and a controlling mechanism. In addition there must be some way of feeding energy in the form of an impetus to the escape

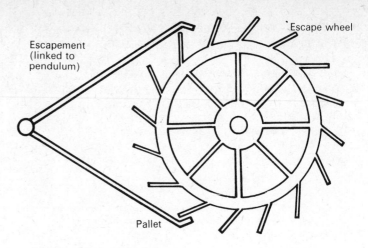

An escapement mechanism

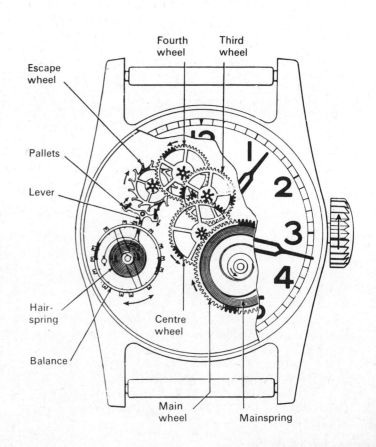

46

wheel so that it keeps rotating. These rotations are then recorded through the hands of the timekeeper.

The controlling mechanism in a watch is not a pendulum but a balance spring. Robert Hooke (page 55) is credited with the invention of the hairspring or balance spring. He discovered that a vibrating spring has a regular rhythm and employed the famous clockmaker Thomas Tompion (page 55) to build him a watch using a vibrating spring as a regulator.

The value of the balance spring, like that of the pendulum, lies in its isochronous (constant timekeeping) effect. It is so useful that it was soon used in portable timekeepers. These, until this time, had been objects of great beauty but uncertain reliability. The first watches to employ a balance spring suffered from considerable friction at their bearings. It was also difficult for craftsmen of that time to produce springs that were exactly the same thickness along the whole of their length.

The use of jewels for bearings was invented by by Nicholas Facio, a Swiss who lived in London at the beginning of the eighteenth century, and it remained a carefully guarded secret amongst a small group of English craftsmen through most of that time. The jewels used were usually sapphires, diamonds and rubies. Today industrially produced gems are widely used : the actual jewels in a jewelled watch are of little intrinsic value.

The balance spring, like the pendulum, is affected by temperature. When it is hot the spring is weaker than normal and when it is cold the spring is stronger than normal. Thus, since the movement of a balance depends on the strength of the spring, it will vibrate more slowly when the temperature rises and more quickly when it falls. Watches were therefore fitted with 'curb pins' which allowed the wearer to alter the length of the spring and compensate for a change in temperature.

Quartz clocks and atomic clocks

Modern clocks, which are used in experiments in space, need to be very accurate indeed. The quartz crystal clock is so accurate that it only gains or loses a second or two in every fifty years. When an electric current is passed through a quartz crystal, the crystal vibrates at a constant rate. A thinner crystal vibrates more quickly than a thick one. These crystals are used as regulators in the quartz crystal clocks. The crystal in a quartz clock is so thin that it vibrates at 1 000 000 times per second. This means that it is possible to measure a few thousandths of a second. Modern space scientists need to be as accurate as that.

The atomic clock is even more accurate. It gains or loses no more than one second every 1 000 years. The atoms in the metal caesium vibrate very regularly and rapidly when the metal is vaporised. These atoms are used as regulators in the atomic clock. These clocks are so accurate that they show that the earth is slowing down.

Atomic clocks are used to correct quartz clocks.

The NPL caesium atomic clock is accurate to 2 parts in 10^{12} or approximately $0.2 \, \mu s/day$. The atomic beam chamber on the right-hand side of the photograph incorporates a double beam system. The racks contain control and measuring equipment.

Some famous clocks

Probably the oldest clocks extant in Britain are those of Salisbury and Wells cathedrals. The original working mechanism of the latter is now housed at the Science Museum in London. Both clocks originally contained foliot balances but were converted to take pendulums. The clock at Salisbury cathedral was refitted with a foliot balance during its restoration, which was completed in 1956.

The famous astronomical clock at Hampton Court in England was made in 1540 for Henry VIII and gives not only the hours, but the phases of the moon, the months and the signs of the zodiac.

A facsimile of Hampton Court clock face

Standard time

Noon for any one place on the earth's surface occurs when the sun is directly over the meridian which passes through that place. Because of the curvature of the earth and its movement from west to east, meridians to the east of any place have already passed through noon; those to the west are yet to get their noon. All places on the same meridian have noon at the same time. Places on other meridians will have noon a different time. Mean solar time at any fixed place on the earth's surface is called its *local time.*

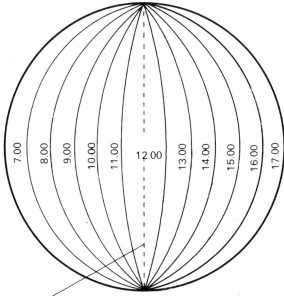

Greenwich meridian 0°

The earth turns through 15° of longitude in every hour. Thus when it is noon at Greenwich, England, it is nearly midnight in Wellington, New Zealand, which is 175° east of Greenwich. Bristol is 180 km west of London and its local time is about ten minutes behind that of London. Even within a large city such as London, it is easy to see that one might be a minute or so different in time from a friend living about a few kilometres away and could possibly be either late or early for an appointment with him. Because

of this, people in the past living in a city or village used their own local time and all clocks in that area agreed. With industrialisation, increased travel and the growth of the railways, a system based on local time was of little use. In Great Britain and Ireland the local time at Greenwich (London) became the standard time (Greenwich Mean Time) in 1880. In the USA and Canada the railways themselves introduced standard time specifying definite junction points where changes in time should be made.

In 1884 an international congress met in Washington, the outcome of whose deliberations was to divide the world into zones, each covering 15° of longitude. The time for each zone was that of the meridian passing through its approximate centre. It differs in time from adjacent zones by one hour. The meridian passing through the observatory at Greenwich was adopted as the zero meridian. This plan was gradually adopted by most nations. The zones were adopted to suit the geographical and political boundaries.

It is interesting that the USA is so large that it has four standard time zones.

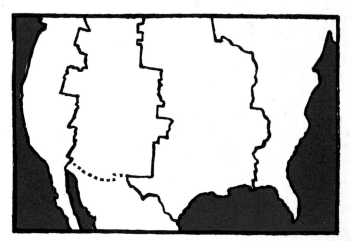

Eight hours
behind Greenwich

Five hours
behind Greenwich

The boundaries do not follow the exact course of the meridians but rather, for practical convenience, join up the terminal or division points used by the railways or follow state borders.

In its apparent journey round the earth the sun takes noon to points west. Gradually it approaches its starting point, bringing noon of the next day with it. Somewhere on its passage round the world, noon of one day changes to noon of the next. This happens when the sun crosses the 180th meridian, which passes through the Pacific Ocean. This meridian is called the International Date Line. When ships cross it going east they must move the calendar back one day and when going west they must move it forward one day.

Places and time

Greenwich

In 1675, King Charles II ordered an observatory to be built to chart the sky and thus make the navigation of his ships easier. The Observatory and a large house for the Astronomer Royal were built at Greenwich by Christopher Wren. Bricks, iron and lead from the Tower of London and a fort at Tilbury were used and £520 towards the cost was obtained by the sale of spoilt gunpowder. The first occupant was Flamsteed, appointed at £100 a year but having to find his own instruments. Indeed he had only two small telescopes and a 3-ft sextant. Since Flamsteed's appointment, Hadley, Bradley, Bliss, Airey, Maskelyne and others have occupied the premises adding both to the equipment and the buildings and bringing great prestige to the office of Astronomer Royal.

Here longitude and latitude were put on a firm basis, the stars were accurately plotted and it was discovered that the earth wobbles at the poles. Through this place runs the Prime Meridian of the world, from which standard time is measured. The Observatory has now been turned into a

Octagon Room, Royal Observatory, Greenwich 1717

museum and on show are not one meridian but three. Flamsteed marked the first one in 1681, then Bradley marked a meridian to the east of this in 1750. The present meridian was marked by Airey in 1850. Astronomical observations are now carried out from Herstmonceux in Sussex where the Observatory had moved by 1958. An allowance is made for the difference in longitude between Greenwich and Herstmonceux.

The Octagon Room as it is today

A large transit telescope was used to observe selected stars as they crossed the Greenwich meridian and the time they did so was noted on a chronograph. The standard clocks at the Royal Observatory were quartz crystal clocks. Signals from the quartz clock were recorded on the chronograph at the same time as the records from the transit telescope, and any difference between the two were noted. The passage of stars across the meridian was observed by eye until as recently as 1956. In that year a photo-zenith tube was introduced which recorded photographically, thus reducing errors due to the observer.

Crystals of quartz, when electrically stimulated, vibrate with a frequency that is extremely regular and the daily variations in the quartz clock are less than one millisecond. The Royal Observatory's quartz clock supplies the 'six-dot-seconds' sent out by the BBC and the time signals which radiate from the GPO's radio station at Rugby.

Ships

The day on board ship is divided into six equal watches of four hours' duration. The watch from 16.00 hours to 20.00 hours is divided into two watches, each two hours long called the dog watches. The purpose of these watches was to allow the crew a change in their sleeping times each day. In the watch and watch system, that is four hours on and four hours off, one 'watch' would be on duty from 00.00–04.00; 08.00 to 12.00; 16.00 to 18.00; 20.00 to 24.00. They would therefore be off duty and normally able to sleep in one spell of four hours (00.00—04.00) one night and in two spells of four hours (20.00—24.00 and 04.00—08.00) the next night and so on. Nowadays there are three 'watches' instead of two and they are on watch at the same time every day.

During the eighteenth century each half-hour of the watch was timed by means of a sand-glass and the custom developed of striking a bell each time the sand-glass emptied. Consequently, at the end of the first half-hour of a watch one bell would be struck, after an hour two bells, and so on, up to eight

bells at the end of a four-hour watch. The strokes are sounded in pairs with an interval between each pair.

British ships follow a special ritual in the dog-watch which stems from a historical event. In 1797 the sailors' dissatisfaction with living conditions on board ship was so intense that they mutinied at the Nore. The signal for the mutiny was five bells in the dog-watch. Since this time the normal bells are struck between 1600 hours and 18.00 hours, but at 18.30 hours only one bell is struck instead of five. The numbering then follows as two bells at 1900 hours, three bells at 19.30 hours and the full eight bells at 20.00 hours. Thus the signal that caused the mutiny has never been repeated.

Biological clocks

Day and night bring with them changes in temperature, light and humidity. The moon and the sun by their gravitational pull cause the rising and falling of the tides which has a profound effect in constantly changing the environment for those organisms which lie in the inter-tidal zone. Affected by such changes, many plants and animals show a regular rhythm in their behaviour; they have evolved 'biological clocks'.

In spring the common cabbage white butterfly emerges from its chrysalis and prepares for flight; this happens not to one but to many butterflies over a large geographical area at this time. Birds sing, court and nest each spring. The Canadian snow-shoe rabbit changes its coat colour for the winter. On a shorter time-scale the fiddler crab's shell grows darker during the day and paler at night, the maximum darkening occurring a little later each day because it is closely bound up with the tides; bean seedlings elevate their leaves during the day and allow them to droop at night; and many flowers open and close to a regular rhythm.

These rhythms take various forms. The behaviour

of birds in spring is an *annual rhythm;* the feeding activity of barnacles, periwinkles and sea anemones once covered by the sea is a *tidal rhythm;* the Palolo worm of the south-western Pacific swarms, in order to breed, in October and November at the third quarter of the moon—this is a *lunar rhythm;* animals active by day or by night show a *diurnal* or *nocturnal rhythm;* and there are even very short rhythms ; for example, the lugworn, common on many sandy shores, moves back and forth in its V-shaped burrow at forty-minute intervals.

The rhythm in man, his solar-day clock, is shown by his pattern of sleeping and waking, of urine production and daily temperature variation. It is very evident when he flies by plane. Flying from London to New York he will get himself five hours out of step with his normal pattern of activities. Studies have shown that people who traverse time zones in this way become irritable and less efficient in their activities. It can even, in some cases, slow their 'reaction time' and this is, of course, important in such things as driving a car.

The way in which biological clocks function is obscure but it is known that light may sometimes play a part. The Canadian snow-shoe rabbit begins to change colour in August and this is linked up with the shortening daylight hours. If the animal is blindfolded for part of the light hours it can be induced to change colour many weeks before it would normally do so. Bean seedlings which elevate their leaves about daybreak may have this pattern upset by subjecting them to a few sessions of darkness by day and illumination by night. After such treatment they will elevate their leaves about the time of sunset.

All living things act in a way that suggests they have clock systems that enable them to register the periods of the day, tide, month or year. How these 'clocks' work is not known ; they do not seem, by and large, to depend directly on changes in light or temperature, but they do give a certain advantage to organisms possessing them.

People and time

Galileo Galilei, 1564–1642
Galileo, one of the greatest of scientists, was born at Pisa on February 15th, 1564.

Galileo

So great was this man that the present synopsis can do no more than bring out those aspects of his work especially concerned with time.

One of Galileo's most famous discoveries is that of the isochronous property of a pendulum. Legend or fact, the story has it that Galileo, as an eighteen-year-old student, was attending a service in the Cathedral of Pisa when one of the attendants drew down the bronze lamp made by Possenti in order to set it alight. In allowing it to return to its position he set it swinging and this began to engage Galileo's interest. He noticed that the oscillations of the lamp gradually died down : as they did so he timed them using his pulse and found they all took the same length of time. (Such an operation is no easy task, as you may see if you try for yourself.) Leading from this discovery, Galileo constructed some devices which could be used for timing the pulse and hence find any variation in its rate. These were used by the physicians of the time and were termed Pulsilogia. Santoria, Professor of Medicine at Padua, in his book *Methodi Vitandorum Erronum in Arte Medica*, published at Venice in 1607, shows different forms of this instrument, two of which are reproduced below.

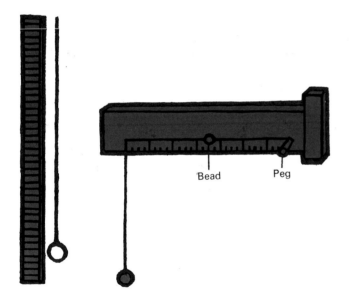

'Bead   Peg

The first of these is a simple pendulum with a graduated scale alongside. The length of the pendulum is shortened or increased until its period of swing coincides with the pulse rate of the patient. A reading can then be taken from the scale. The shorter the pendulum the more rapid the pulse rate, the longer the pendulum the slower the pulse rate.

The second Pulsilogia has the pendulum and scale connected. The length of the pendulum can be adjusted by turning the peg and the scale can be read off by means of the bead attached to the string.

In 1610 Galileo discovered the satellites of Jupiter or, it is more correct to say, his telescope was powerful enough to show four of them, the other eight being found in the late nineteenth or early twentieth century. He spent six years observing and calculating their movement. As they rotate around Jupiter they are frequently eclipsed by the planet and Galileo worked out a method of predicting these eclipses. He then reasoned that a mariner at sea could compare the time of local noon with the time mentioned in his tables for the eclipse of Jupiter's satellites and thus determine his longitude. For example, if the seaman notes an eclipse at 5 h 9 min 10 s local time and finds that it was due to occur at Greenwich at 7 h 39 min 10 s ($2\frac{1}{2}$ h later) then he knows he is :

$$\frac{360° \times 2\frac{1}{2}}{24} = 37° \ 30' \text{ east of Greenwich.}$$

There were inherent difficulties, to say the least, in such a method. The motion of the ship would upset the observer, Jupiter is often so near the sun that it is difficult to observe the eclipses, and the timekeepers of the day were so inaccurate that it would be difficult to keep a reasonable record of the time from local noon until the observation of the time of the elipse. Galileo made an attempt to rectify these deficiencies. He devised a binocular telescope that he called the Celatone or Testiera, a device something like a gas-mask that fitted on the observer's head and had a telescope mounted rigidly in each eye. Galileo also had a chair made at the arsenal at Pisa which floated in a container filled with water and in which the observer would be protected from the ship's motion. The Spanish and Dutch governments had offered prizes for the discovery of a method of determining longitude at sea and Galileo offered his discovery to them but the negotiations just dragged on and were never brought to a final conclusion—a matter not surprising in view of the practical difficulties involved.

Over half a century after Galileo's discovery of the properties of a pendulum his mind turned to its application to clocks. He, of course, realised the value of the pendulum as a timing device and had employed it as such in his Pulsilogia. But in 1641 his thoughts dwelt on using it as a regulator for a mechanical clock. Vincenzio, Galileo's son made a drawing from his father's dictation but Galileo fell ill and died before the clock could be made. Vincenzio returned to the task several years later but he too died before he completed his work. The honour of making the first pendulum clock belongs to Christian Huygens.

Galileo's pendulum

The story of Galileo is both fascinating and tragic. At the age of seventy and in a poor state of health he was summoned to appear before the Inquisition at Rome and recant, on bended knee, the Copernican doctrine that the earth moves round the sun with a diurnal motion, a doctrine which he had upheld and collected much evidence for over a period of thirty years. It is often cited that Galileo, as he rose from his knees, murmured 'Eppur si muove' ('It moves, nevertheless'). It is doubtful, whether so old and so ill a man who had suffered a trial lasting almost a year would have done this, especially in view of the thoroughness of his recantation, but it is heartwarming to think that he might.

Christian Huygens, 1629–1695

Christian Huygens was born at the Hague, the son of a gifted father, Constantyn, secretary to the Prince of Orange. Christian entered the University of Leyden at the age of sixteen and two years later moved to the University of Breda, studying mathematics and law.

Huygens became a noted scientist, and, like Galileo, his interests were many. He discovered the rings of Saturn and Saturn's largest satellite. Much of his life was spent in Paris, where he helped in setting up, and participated in, the Royal Academy of Science.

To Huygens must go the credit for applying the pendulum as a regulator in clocks and also the credit for working out the mathematical theory behind the movement of a pendulum. He spent a great deal of time between 1655 and 1660 in developing a pendulum clock. The first one was made in 1657. In 1658 Huygens published a book, *Horologium*, in which he describes a pendulum clock and which led in 1673 to the publishing of his great work *Horologium Oscillatorium*. The latter not only discusses the construction and use of a pendulum clock but considers oscillation in a cycloidal arc, centrifugal force and the measurement of curves.

Huygens, in his study of the pendulum, had found that its period of swing was not independent of the arc (that is to say, a very wide swing will take a slightly longer time than a narrow swing) and he therefore designed a pair of curved metal plates or cheeks to correct the period for large swings of the pendulum. The pendulum was suspended from a pair of cords slung between these cheeks. This idea was soon abandoned because of the difficulties it caused when put into practice.

In 1659 Huygens began development of a timekeeper for use at sea and hence of value in determining longitude. In 1674 he scrapped earlier designs for this and produced one with a balance wheel and balance spring. This action led to the irascible Robert Hooke claiming that Huygens had learned of the use of a spring through Oldenburg, the secretary of the Royal Society, and had pirated the device. It seems there could be little truth in Hooke's claim, for Huygen's use of the spring differed from that of Hooke. Hooke's spring allowed the balance to move through an arc of 120° whilst Huygen's balance made several turns at each beat.

Robert Hooke, 1635–1703
Robert Hooke was born the son of a curate in the parish of Freshwater on the Isle of Wight. He proved so clever that by the age of twenty he had become attached, at a salary, to the famous scientist Robert Boyle at Oxford. No portraits of Hooke exist, but that delicious gossip of the age, Aubrey, furnishes us with a description that would better many a painter's work, 'Of middling stature, somewhat crooked, pale-faced and his face but little belowe, but his head is large : his eie is full and popping, and not quick ; a grey eie. He had a delicate head of haire, browne, and of an excellent moist curle. He is and ever was very temperate and moderate in dyet, etc. As he is of prodigious inventive head, he is a person of great virtue and goodness.'

He was undoubtedly a great figure of his times, with a mind interested not only in science but also in painting, languages and mathematics as well. He explored most aspects of science known at that time, produced many inventions and poured forth suggestions. Part of his trouble was that he never delved long enough into specific aspects, but would be restlessly moving from subject to subject. He was also a vain and suspicious man, given to quarrelling.

His notable contribution in the field of time is the development of the balance or hairspring. He was appointed curator of the Royal Society in 1662, and since he was not a wealthy man Sir John Cutler instituted a lectureship of £50 a year for his benefit. During the Cutlerian lectures of 1664 he outlined the methods of applying springs to a watch's balance, thus making its motion more uniform. Scientists of the age, amongst whom were Galileo, Newton and Huygens, adopted a curious method of establishing a prior claim to an invention without disclosing its nature. This was to publish their discovery in the form of an anagram. This Hooke did for his discovery of the principle of a balance spring. The anagram ran c, e, i, i, i, n, o, s, s, s, t, t, u, v, which gives the Latin 'Ut tensio, sic vis'—'as the tension is, so is the force'. That is, the force exerted by the spring is proportional to the extent it is put under tension.

Robert Hooke employed the famous clockmaker Thomas Tompion to make watches using his balance spring.

Thomas Tompion, 1638–1713
Thomas Tompion, who was often described as the Father of English Clockmaking, was born at Ickfield Green in Bedfordshire, the son of a blacksmith. Little is known of his early life but in 1671 he was admitted to the Clockmakers' Company. At the time, he was referred to as a 'Great Clockmaker', which meant that he specialised in building large turret or church clocks.

Tompion made friends with Robert Hooke early in his career and executed work for him. His first task for Robert Hooke was the making, not of a clock or watch, but of a quadrant which the Royal Society had commissioned. Much of what is known of Tompion is gained from Hooke's diaries and it says a great deal of Tompion that he managed to keep the friendship of so irascible a character as Dr Hooke throughout Hooke's lifetime.

Watches, at the time Tompion began his career, were very inaccurate and were usually highly ornamental in appearance since they were worn in full view. At Tompion's death the watch had developed into an efficient mechanism; a fact due in no small measure to Tompion himself. One of the overriding factors in this development was the invention of the balance spring. Hooke had demonstrated the value of the balance spring as an isochronous device but had suppressed his invention until, in February 1675, he obtained news of a 'pendulum watch' devised by the Dutch scientist Christian Huygens, which was controlled by a spring. Furious that his invention should be claimed by another, he engaged Tompion to produce for him a watch controlled by a balance spring. Tompion completed the watch by April of that year and accompanied Hooke and Sir Jonas More (a noted mathematician of the time) to show the watch to King Charles II. As Hooke noted 'With the King and shewd him my new spring watch, Sir J. More and Tompion there. The King most graciously pleased with it and commended it far beyond Zulichens' (Christian Huygen van Zulichen). Charles ordered a watch for his own use which Tompion duly completed and which illustrates Robert Hooke's obsession with his discovery, for it was inscribed 'R. Hook inven 1658. T. Tompion fecit 1675'.

Travelling clock made by Tompion, 1700

The incorporation of the balance spring in the watch rendered other changes necessary in watches and these Tompion successfully achieved. He grew to be a man of substance, employing a large number of workmen and turning out work of a consistently high quality and accuracy; so much so that fraudulent imitations were made of his watches.

Sir Jonas More commissioned two clocks from Tompion for the new Observatory at Greenwich, and the first Astronomer Royal, Flamsteed, noted: 'My pendulum clocks were the work of Mr. Tompion: the pendulum, thirteen feet long, make each single vibration in two seconds of time; and their weights need only to be drawn up once in twelve months.'

Tompion executed work for Charles II, William III and Queen Anne and frequently visited the palaces to check the timing of his clocks. Indeed, William III's extravagance gave Tompion free range of his imagination and skill and he produced some of the world's most superb clocks for this monarch.

Tompion died in 1713, having brought the watch to as near perfection as was possible then. He was buried at Westminster Abbey.

John Harrison, 1693–1776
The following account owes much to the excellent writings on John Harrison in R. T. Gould's fascinating book on the marine chronometer. John Harrison, the son of a carpenter, was born at Foulby in the parish of Wragby, Yorkshire, in 1693.

His lifelong interest, and major work, was to devise a timekeeper of great accuracy for telling the time at sea. Nations had always realised that the safe passage of their ships at sea depended upon the ships being able to determine their longitude with a high degree of accuracy. Latitude could be calculated fairly easily by determining the angle of elevation of the sun at noon, but longitude could only be got by comparing the ship's local noon with the time of noon at a chosen fixed meridian. Since the Royal Observatory was at Greenwich it was natural to take noon at Greenwich as the time of reference. The problem could easily be solved if there was a clock on board ship giving *accurately* the time at Greenwich.

Nowadays one tends to forget how chancy navigation at sea must have been in those times and why there was a high percentage of shipwrecks. So vital was the problem that the Board of Longitude in London offered an unprecedented amount of money for such times 'for providing a reward for such person or persons as shall discover the longitude'. This was done in 1714 and they offered £10 000 if within 1° (60 geographical miles), £15 000 if within 2-3° (40 miles) and £20 000 if within ½° (30 miles).

Such a project and such a reward fired John Harrison's imagination and enthusiasm. In 1728 he came to London with a drawing of the marine clock he wanted to build and was lucky enough to find a friend in George Graham, who not only

advised him to build his timekeeper before applying to the Board of Longitude but also loaned him money to do so. Harrison went back to Barrow upon Humber and spent all his spare time on completing his clock. It took six years and the clock (now preserved at Greenwich) when completed weighed 72 lb (32.5 kg) and stood 2 ft × 2 ft × 1½ ft (60 cm × 60 cm × 45 cm). Instead of a pendulum it had two very large balances which swung in opposite directions simultaneously. The motive force for the clock was provided by two large springs and Harrison incorporated his grasshopper escapement into the mechanism.

In 1735 the Board of Longitude ordered a trial and Harrison journeyed to Lisbon on board HMS *Centurion* and returned in HMS *Orford*. The value of the clock was undoubted as is shown by the following certificate written by Roger Wills, master of the *Orford:*

'When we made land, the said land, according to my reckoning (and others), ought to have been the Start, but, before we knew what land it was, John Harrison declared to me and the rest of the ship's company that, according to his observations with his machine, it ought to be the Lizard—the which, indeed, it was found to be, his observation showing the ship to be more west than my reckoning, above one degree and twenty-six miles !'

It is easy to see, if a map is consulted, that the voyage was almost north–south and a more stringent test would be needed. Furthermore, the Act of Queen Anne, under which the reward was to be given, specified a trip to the West Indies. The Board of Longitude gave Harrison £500 to continue his work and he made a second clock which he completed by 1739. This was not tried out, however, because England was at war with Spain and it might well have fallen into the wrong hands.

Harrison began work on a third timekeeper and took over seventeen years on this, completing it in 1757. He then suggested making a fourth timekeeper and this was finished by 1759. It is a most beautiful thing, only 5 in (13 cm) in diameter and in the form of a large pair-cased silver watch. Harrison had spent over fifty years on this labour of love. It was to be tried out in 1761.

Harrison's chronometer

Harrison, who was now seventy-six, could not travel with it and his son, William, was sent on HMS *Deptford* to the West Indies. The timekeeper was put in a case with four locks and these were entrusted to various people on board ship.

The ship sailed from Spithead on November, 18th 1761. Dudley Digges, the ship's captain, reckoned after nine days' sailing that the ship was 13° 50' west of Greenwich, but William Harrison found from his reckoning, using the timekeeper, that the ship was 15° 15' west. Digges offered to bet him five to one he was wrong but held the ship to its course. Harrison was rewarded by the sighting of Porto Santo, the north-east island of the Madeira group at 6 am the next day, an occurrence that he had predicted. The ship's company showed some enthusiasm for the result too, for if they had missed Madeira it 'would have been inconvenient, as they were in Want of Beer'.

The result of the voyage was to show the timekeeper to be accurate within 11' of longitude, a finding extraordinarily well within the limits laid down by the Board of Longitude. However, the prize was too large for the Board to grant without further tests but an interim sum of £2,500 was given.

Further trials at sea lasting 156 days showed an error of less than one-tenth of a second per day. The Board still declined to pay, one of their reasons being that they had not been given sufficient details of the workings of the timekeeper. A battle royal in the literal sense began with John Harrison supported by George III, who had taken a great interest in the matter. In April 1772 Harrison petitioned Parliament and was supported by, amongst others, Charles Fox. A bill was passed which resulted in the total moneys paid to Harrison reaching £22,550.

Harrison—'Longitude Harrison'—as he was called, died in 1776, aged eighty-three. He was a great Englishman whose toil did much that helped this maritime nation and sailors throughout the world.

It is interesting to note that one Larcum Kendall made two copies of his 'sea-clock' as Harrison termed it. One was used by Captain Cook on his second voyage of discovery and the other belonged to Captain Bligh of the *Bounty*.

With objectives in mind

With objectives in mind (the background book for the project) discusses some of the objectives that are pertinent to science and that might be attained by children. It distributes these objectives among stages that refer to the development of children. The following are some of these objectives as they relate to this Unit on *Time*.

Stage 1
Willing participation in group work.

Awareness that there are various ways of testing out ideas and making observations.

Awareness that more than one variable may be involved in a particular change.

Appreciation of the need for measurement.

These objectives, amongst others, are relevant to the stage where children are beginning to manipulate things mentally. In devising simple clocks they will probably work in groups, they will certainly find that more than one variable is involved in a particular change (for example, that both height of water and size of aperture affect the emptying of a water clock); they will find that some clocks empty more quickly than others and they will begin to appreciate the need for measurement.

At Stage 2 children's mental manipulations are becoming more varied and powerful and this is expressed in the objectives:

Stage 2
Enjoyment in developing methods for solving problems or testing ideas.

Ability to frame questions likely to be answered through investigations.

Awareness of some discoveries and inventions of famous scientists.

Children at this stage often tend to have problems that are particularly their own. Interest in shadows, for example, may lead to devising methods of finding out about them. Such methods will inevitably involve measurement. The idea of the movement of shadows being used as a clock may emerge and perhaps lead to study and investigation of other clocks and of the men who developed them.

The objectives relevant at Stages 1 and 2 to *Time* are many. They are engendered in the following general objectives that children might profitably achieve:

Awareness of methods of measuring time and ability to use them.

Awareness of famous people concerned in the development of time-measuring devices.

Awareness of time around the world.

Awareness of, and ability to investigate, factors in the environment that change with the passage of time.

Awareness of, and ability to investigate, the time of response of one's body to a stimulus.

Awareness of biological 'clocks'.

Reference material

The following books may interest those who wish to study the subject in greater depth:

Bell, A. E., *Christian Huygens*, 1947.
Brown, F. A., *Biological Clocks*, 1962.
Chamberlain, Paul M., *It's About Time*, 1941.
Encyclopaedia Britannica
Fahie, J. S., *Galileo, His Life and Work*, 1903.
Gould, R. T., *The Marine Chronometer*, 1923.
Gould, R. T., *John Harrison and his Timekeepers*, Science Museum, 1935.
Hawkins, G. S., *Stonehenge Decoded*, Fontana, 1970.
Herbert, A. P., *Sundials Old and New*, 1967.
Nillson, M. P., *Primitive Time Reckoning*, 1923.
Nuffield Mathematics, *Beginnings 1*.
Nuffield Mathematics, *Computation and Structure 2*.
Symonds, R. W., *Thomas Tompion, His Life and Work*, 1951.
Ward, F. A. B., *Time Measurement, Part 1, Historical Review*, 1961.
Ward, F. A. B., *Time Measurement, Descriptive Catalogue of the Science Museum Collection*, 1966.
Whitaker's Almanack.
USA Bureau of Standards, *Standard Time throughout the World*, Pamphlet (Circular No. 339), 1932.

Books for children

Adler, J., *Time in Your Life*, 1957.
Goudsmit, S. A., and Clairborne, R., *Time*, 1967.
Llin, M., *What Time Is It?*, 1932.
Hood, P., *How Time is Measured*, 2nd edition, 1969.
Razzell and Watts, *Have We Got Time?*, 1970.
Ward, F. A. B., *Timekeepers*, Science Museum Illustrated Booklet, 1963.
Macdonald Junior Reference Library 56, *Time and Timepieces*.

Chart
Time Zone Chart published by the Admiralty and available from J. D. Potter Ltd, 145 Minories, London, EC3.

Candle
King Alfred Candle—Michael L. Beach, 41 Church Street, Twickenham.

Filmstrip
Keeping Time N149.
The British Broadcasting Corporation, The Langham, Portland Place, London, W1.
Accompanying tape-recording from Stagesound Ltd, 11–12 King Street, Covent Garden, London, WC2.

Objectives for children learning science

Guide lines to keep in mind

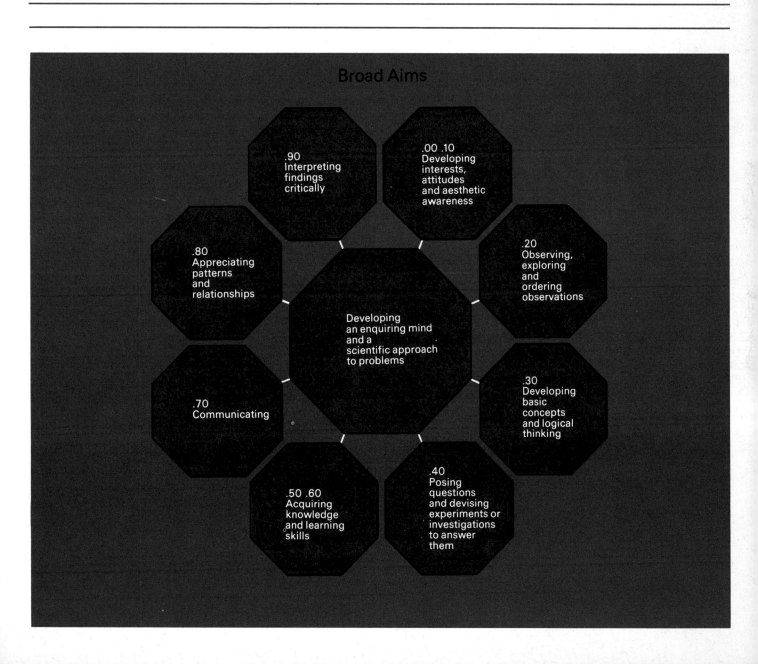

What we mean by Stage 1, Stage 2 and Stage 3

Attitudes, interests and aesthetic awareness

.00/.10

Stage 1
Transition from intuition to concrete operations. Infants generally.

The characteristics of thought among infant children differ in important respects from those of children over the age of about seven years. Infant thought has been described as 'intuitive' by Piaget; it is closely associated with physical action and is dominated by immediate observation. Generally, the infant is not able to think about or imagine the consequences of an action unless he has actually carried it out, nor is he yet likely to draw logical conclusions from his experiences. At this early stage the objectives are those concerned with active exploration of the immediate environment and the development of ability to discuss and communicate effectively: they relate to the kind of activities that are appropriate to these very young children, and which form an introduction to ways of exploring and of ordering observations.

1.01 Willingness to ask questions
1.02 Willingness to handle both living and non-living material.
1.03 Sensitivity to the need for giving proper care to living things.
1.04 Enjoyment in using all the senses for exploring and discriminating.
1.05 Willingness to collect material for observation or investigation.

Concrete operations. Early stage.

In this Stage, children are developing the ability to manipulate things mentally. At first this ability is limited to objects and materials that can be manipulated concretely, and even then only in a restricted way. The objectives here are concerned with developing these mental operations through exploration of concrete objects and materials—that is to say, objects and materials which, as physical things, have meaning for the child. Since older children, and even adults prefer an introduction to new ideas and problems through concrete example and physical exploration, these objectives are suitable for all children, whatever their age, who are being introduced to certain science activities for the first time.

1.06 Desire to find out things for oneself.
1.07 Willing participation in group work.
1.08 Willing compliance with safety regulations in handling tools and equipment.
1.09 Appreciation of the need to learn the meaning of new words and to use them correctly.

Stage 2
Concrete operations. Later stage.

In this Stage, a continuation of what Piaget calls the stage of concrete operations, the mental manipulations are becoming more varied and powerful. The developing ability to handle variables—for example, in dealing with multiple classification—means that problems can be solved in more ordered and quantitative ways than was previously possible. The objectives begin to be more specific to the exploration of the scientific aspects of the environment rather than to general experience, as previously. These objectives are developments of those of Stage 1 and depend on them for a foundation. They are those thought of as being appropriate for all children who have progressed from Stage 1 and not merely for nine- to eleven-year-olds.

2.01 Willingness to co-operate with others in science activities.
2.02 Willingness to observe objectively.
2.03 Appreciation of the reasons for safety regulations.
2.04 Enjoyment in examining ambiguity in the use of words.
2.05 Interest in choosing suitable means of expressing results and observations.
2.06 Willingness to assume responsibility for the proper care of living things.
2.07 Willingness to examine critically the results of their own and others' work.
2.08 Preference for putting ideas to test before accepting or rejecting them.
2.09 Appreciation that approximate methods of comparison may be more appropriate than careful measurements.

Stage 3
Transition to stage of abstract thinking.

This is the Stage in which, for some children, the ability to think about abstractions is developing. When this development is complete their thought is capable of dealing with the possible and hypothetical, and is not tied to the concrete and to the here and now. It may take place between eleven and thirteen for some able children, for some children it may happen later, and for others it may never occur. The objectives of this stage are ones which involve development of ability to use hypothetical reasoning and to separate and combine variables in a systematic way. They are appropriate to those who have achieved most of the Stage 2 objectives and who now show signs of ability to manipulate mentally ideas and propositions.

3.01 Acceptance of responsibility for their own and others' safety in experiments.
3.02 Preference for using words correctly.
3.03 Commitment to the idea of physical cause and effect.
3.04 Recognition of the need to standardise measurements.
3.05 Willingness to examine evidence critically.
3.06 Willingness to consider beforehand the usefulness of the results from a possible experiment.
3.07 Preference for choosing the most appropriate means of expressing results or observations.
3.08 Recognition of the need to acquire new skills.
3.09 Willingness to consider the role of science in everyday life.

Attitudes, interests and aesthetic awareness

.00/.10

Observing, exploring and ordering observations

.20

1.21 Appreciation of the variety of living things and materials in the environment.
1.22 Awareness of changes which take place as time passes.
1.23 Recognition of common shapes—square, circle, triangle.
1.24 Recognition of regularity in patterns.
1.25 Ability to group things consistently according to chosen or given criteria.

1.11 Awareness that there are various ways of testing out ideas and making observations.
1.12 Interest in comparing and classifying living or non-living things.
1.13 Enjoyment in comparing measurements with estimates.
1.14 Awareness that there are various ways of expressing results and observations.
1.15 Willingness to wait and to keep records in order to observe change in things.
1.16 Enjoyment in exploring the variety of living things in the environment.
1.17 Interest in discussing and comparing the aesthetic qualities of materials.

1.26 Awareness of the structure and form of living things.
1.27 Awareness of change of living things and non-living materials.
1.28 Recognition of the action of force.
1.29 Ability to group living and non-living things by observable attributes.
1.29a Ability to distinguish regularity in events and motion.

2.11 Enjoyment in developing methods for solving problems or testing ideas.
2.12 Appreciation of the part that aesthetic qualities of materials play in determining their use.
2.13 Interest in the way discoveries were made in the past.

2.21 Awareness of internal structure in living and non-living things.
2.22 Ability to construct and use keys for identification.
2.23 Recognition of similar and congruent shapes.
2.24 Awareness of symmetry in shapes and structures.
2.25 Ability to classify living things and non-living materials in different ways.
2.26 Ability to visualise objects from different angles and the shape of cross-sections.

3.11 Appreciation of the main principles in the care of living things.
3.12 Willingness to extend methods used in science activities to other fields of experience.

3.21 Appreciation that classification criteria are arbitrary.
3.22 Ability to distinguish observations which are relevant to the solution of a problem from those which are not.
3.23 Ability to estimate the order of magnitude of physical quantities.

	Developing basic concepts and logical thinking .30	Posing questions and devising experiments or investigations to answer them .40
Stage 1 Transition from intuition to concrete operations. Infants generally.	1.31 Awareness of the meaning of words which describe various types of quantity. 1.32 Appreciation that things which are different may have features in common.	1.41 Ability to find answers to simple problems by investigation. 1.42 Ability to make comparisons in terms of one property or variable.
Concrete operations. Early stage.	1.33 Ability to predict the effect of certain changes through observation of similar changes. 1.34 Formation of the notions of the horizontal and the vertical. 1.35 Development of concepts of conservation of length and substance. 1.36 Awareness of the meaning of speed and of its relation to distance covered.	1.43 Appreciation of the need for measurement. 1.44 Awareness that more than one variable may be involved in a particular change.
Stage 2 Concrete operations. Later stage.	2.31 Appreciation of measurement as division into regular parts and repeated comparison with a unit. 2.32 Appreciation that comparisons can be made indirectly by use of an intermediary. 2.33 Development of concepts of conservation of weight, area and volume. 2.34 Appreciation of weight as a downward force. 2.35 Understanding of the speed, time, distance relation.	2.41 Ability to frame questions likely to be answered through investigations. 2.42 Ability to investigate variables and to discover effective ones. 2.43 Appreciation of the need to control variables and use controls in investigations. 2.44 Ability to choose and use either arbitrary or standard units of measurement as appropriate. 2.45 Ability to select a suitable degree of approximation and work to it. 2.46 Ability to use representational models for investigating problems or relationships.
Stage 3 Transition to stage of abstract thinking.	3.31 Familiarity with relationships involving velocity, distance, time, acceleration. 3.32 Ability to separate, exclude or combine variables in approaching problems. 3.33 Ability to formulate hypotheses not dependent upon direct observation. 3.34 Ability to extend reasoning beyond the actual to the possible. 3.35 Ability to distinguish a logically sound proof from others less sound.	3.41 Attempting to identify the essential steps in approaching a problem scientifically. 3.42 Ability to design experiments with effective controls for testing hypotheses. 3.43 Ability to visualise a hypothetical situation as a useful simplification of actual observations. 3.44 Ability to construct scale models for investigation and to appreciate implications of changing the scale.

1.51 Ability to discriminate between different materials.
1.52 Awareness of the characteristics of living things.
1.53 Awareness of properties which materials can have.
1.54 Ability to use displayed reference material for identifying living and non-living things.

1.55 Familiarity with sources of sound.
1.56 Awareness of sources of heat, light and electricity.
1.57 Knowledge that change can be produced in common substances.
1.58 Appreciation that ability to move or cause movement requires energy.
1.59 Knowledge of differences in properties between and within common groups of materials.

1.61 Appreciation of man's use of other living things and their products.
1.62 Awareness that man's way of life has changed through the ages.
1.63 Skill in manipulating tools and materials.
1.64 Development of techniques for handling living things correctly.
1.65 Ability to use books for supplementing ideas or information.

2.51 Knowledge of conditions which promote changes in living things and non-living materials.
2.52 Familiarity with a wide range of forces and of ways in which they can be changed.
2.53 Knowledge of sources and simple properties of common forms of energy.
2.54 Knowledge of the origins of common materials.
2.55 Awareness of some discoveries and inventions by famous scientists.
2.56 Knowledge of ways to investigate and measure properties of living things and non-living materials.
2.57 Awareness of changes in the design of measuring instruments and tools during man's history.
2.58 Skill in devising and constructing simple apparatus.
2.59 Ability to select relevant information from books or other reference material.

3.51 Knowledge that chemical change results from interaction.
3.52 Knowledge that energy can be stored and converted in various ways.
3.53 Awareness of the universal nature of gravity.
3.54 Knowledge of the main constituents and variations in the composition of soil and of the earth.
3.55 Knowledge that properties of matter can be explained by reference to its particulate nature.
3.56 Knowledge of certain properties of heat, light, sound, electrical, mechanical and chemical energy.
3.57 Knowledge of a wide range of living organisms.
3.58 Development of the concept of an internal environment.
3.59 Knowledge of the nature and variations in basic life processes.

3.61 Appreciation of levels of organisation in living things.
3.62 Appreciation of the significance of the work and ideas of some famous scientists.
3.63 Ability to apply relevant knowledge without help of contextual cues.
3.64 Ability to use scientific equipment and instruments for extending the range of human senses.

Communicating	Appreciating patterns and relationships
.70	**.80**

Stage 1
Transition from
intuition to
concrete
operations.
Infants
generally.

Communicating	Appreciating patterns and relationships
1.71 Ability to use new words appropriately.	1.81 Awareness of cause-effect relationships.
1.72 Ability to record events in their sequences.	
1.73 Ability to discuss and record impressions of living and non-living things in the environment.	
1.74 Ability to use representational symbols for recording information on charts or block graphs.	

- -

Concrete
operations.
Early stage.

Communicating	Appreciating patterns and relationships
1.75 Ability to tabulate information and use tables.	1.82 Development of a concept of environment.
1.76 Familiarity with names of living things and non-living materials.	1.83 Formation of a broad idea of variation in living things.
1.77 Ability to record impressions by making models, painting or drawing.	1.84 Awareness of seasonal changes in living things.
	1.85 Awareness of differences in physical conditions between different parts of the Earth.

Stage 2
Concrete
operations.
Later stage.

Communicating	Appreciating patterns and relationships
2.71 Ability to use non-representational symbols in plans, charts, etc.	2.81 Awareness of sequences of change in natural phenomena.
2.72 Ability to interpret observations in terms of trends and rates of change.	2.82 Awareness of structure-function relationship in parts of living things.
2.73 Ability to use histograms and other simple graphical forms for communicating data.	2.83 Appreciation of interdependence among living things.
2.74 Ability to construct models as a means of recording observations.	2.84 Awareness of the impact of man's activities on other living things.
	2.85 Awareness of the changes in the physical environment brought about by man's activity.
	2.86 Appreciation of the relationships of parts and wholes.

Stage 3
Transition to
stage of
abstract
thinking.

Communicating	Appreciating patterns and relationships
3.71 Ability to select the graphical form most appropriate to the information being recorded.	3.81 Recognition that the ratio of volume to surface area is significant.
3.72 Ability to use three-dimensional models or graphs for recording results.	3.82 Appreciation of the scale of the universe.
3.73 Ability to deduce information from graphs : from gradient, area, intercept.	3.83 Understanding of the nature and significance of changes in living and non-living things.
3.74 Ability to use analogies to explain scientific ideas and theories.	3.84 Recognition that energy has many forms and is conserved when it is changed from one form to another.
	3.85 Recognition of man's impact on living things— conservation, change, control.
	3.86 Appreciation of the social implications of man's changing use of materials, historical and contemporary.
	3.87 Appreciation of the social implications of research in science.
	3.88 Appreciation of the role of science in the changing pattern of provision for human needs.

Interpreting findings critically

.90

1.91 Awareness that the apparent size, shape and relationships of things depend on the position of the observer.

- -

1.92 Appreciation that properties of materials influence their use.

2.91 Appreciation of adaptation to environment.
2.92 Appreciation of how the form and structure of materials relate to their function and properties.
2.93 Awareness that many factors need to be considered when choosing a material for a particular use.
2.94 Recognition of the role of chance in making measurements and experiments.

3.91 Ability to draw from observations conclusions that are unbiased by preconception.
3.92 Willingness to accept factual evidence despite preceptual contradictions.
3.93 Awareness that the degree of accuracy of measurements has to be taken into account when results are interpreted.
3.94 Awareness that unstated assumptions can affect conclusions drawn from argument or experimental results.
3.95 Appreciation of the need to integrate findings into a simplifying generalisation.
3.96 Willingness to check that conclusions are consistent with further evidence.

These Stages we have chosen conform to modern ideas about children's learning. They conveniently describe for us the mental development of children between the ages of five and thirteen years, but it must be remembered that ALTHOUGH CHILDREN GO THROUGH THESE STAGES IN THE SAME ORDER THEY DO NOT GO THROUGH THEM AT THE SAME RATES.
SOME children achieve the later Stages at an early age.
SOME loiter in the early Stages for quite a time.
SOME never have the mental ability to develop to the later Stages.
ALL appear to be ragged in their movement from one Stage to another.
Our Stages, then, are not tied to chronological age, so in any one class of children there will be, almost certainly, some children at differing Stages of mental development.

Index

Illustration acknowledgements:

The publishers gratefully acknowledge the help given by the
following in supplying photographs on the pages indicated:

Aerofilms Limited, 36
The directors and trustees of the Science Museum, 38, 43, 44, 48, 54,
 56, 58
The Mansell Collection, 52
The National Maritime Museum, 50
The National Physical Laboratory, 47
All other photographs South West Picture Agency

Line drawings by The Garden Studio: Anna Barnard
Cover design by Peter Gauld

70